Collection
"La ville est belle"

The City of

BAYEUX

Translated by T. Brian Greenhalgh & Michael Greenhalgh, BA (Hons) M. Phil.

Contents

Bayeux is justly renowned the world over for its Tapestry, embroidered in wool on a cloth of linen in the 11th century ; seventy metres long, it illustrates the story of the conquest of England by William, Duke of Normandy. This chef-d'œuvre is not the only part of Bayeux's illustrious heritage.

Founded at the beginning of our Era, capital of some of the richest earth in agricultural France, seat of a great diocese, the City has treasures in architecture, religious edifices and private dwellings that have retained the charm of times past. The Cathedral, both Norman and Gothic, closely intermixed, its timbered houses and manors of the 14th, 15th, and 16th centuries punctuate the passage of those who pass through the alleys in the heart of the medieval city, as with ancient parts that today form a dense urban tissue intimately integrated. Bayeux gives equal fame to two other spheres of creative art : Lace and Porcelain. The finest examples of these can now be seen in the Baron Gérard Museum, the former residence of the Bishops of Bayeux.

Miraculously unscathed after the battle of June 1944, yet within a few kilometres of the Allied Landing beaches, Bayeux has preserved for posterity this vital moment in the History of Europe, thanks to its museums : the Battle of Normandy Memorial and the General de Gaulle Memorial Museum.

A Secondary Capital of the Duchy of Normandy

Bayeux was, with Aregenua (Vieux) and Noviomagus (Lisieux) one of three « cités » of Calvados, founded in the Gallo-Roman period. Under the name of Augustodurum, it was the administrative capital of *pagus Bajocaensis* or « Pays du Bessin », covering the region between the rivers : Orne and Vire. At the end of the 3rd century, Bayeux was surrounded by walls to protect it from the barbarian raids and thus acquired special status in the century following, with the presence of military contingents charged with the defence of the coasts of Normandy, forming the « *litus saxonicum* ». (Saxon frontier).

At this period too, Bayeux became important ecclesiastically, since from the 4th century it was the seat of a Bishop, owing allegiance to the Archbishop of Rouen. The Bishop of Bayeux extended his authority beyond the Orne, including in his diocese a large part of the Viducasses territory, their capital being the old Aregenua.

Becoming part of the Duchy of Normandy in 924, Bayeux became second capital of the Duchy and reached the peak of its importance in the 11th century, particularly in the early decades of the reign of William the Conqueror.

Rue Quincangrogne

5

Queen Matilda embroidering the Tapestry, a romantic vision of work on the chef-d'œuvre by A. Guillard (1848) (Baron Gérard Museum)

The famous Tapestry that the Bishop of Bayeux Odo of Conteville, half-brother of the Duke and King, ordered for his Cathedral, bears witness to its symbolic importance to the City. Bayeux was in fact a great city, energetic prosperous and wealthy. They were proud of the Episcopal Palace built by Odo with its rich interior, the walls adorned with paintings, as also the great mansion of the treasurer to the Chapter, Conan (on the site of the Deanery) and the fine houses of the Canons. Held also in admiration was the new cathedral, its ample proportions and magnificence, dedicated in 1077 in the presence of the King and Queen, and where their own daughter Agatha was buried. She had been betrothed to Harold le Félon, then promised to Alphonso, King of Castille. Noteworthy was the splendour of the furnishings such as the Crown of Light in gilded copperplate covered with leaves of silver, given by Odo, then too, the reliquaries of gold, encrusted with precious stones, within which were the relics of Saints Raven and Rasiphe, all part of the treasure. The beginning of the 12th century however marked the rapid decline of the City, devastated in 1105 by the War of Succession between the sons of the Conqueror : Robert Courtheuse and Henry I (Beauclerc). To economic ruin was added political decline. Temporal power was transferred to the capital being founded by Duke William in Caen, around the two abbeys and the mighty fortress founded in 1060 on the west bank of the Orne.

The new city was of course set up in the old County of Bayeux and its rapid growth confirmed its status. After Normandy became again part of the French Kingdom in 1204, the Bajocassian City was attached to the bailliwick of Caen and was no more than the seat of a viscount, cut off from its lands which extended to the east of the course of the river Seulles.

In this, Bayeux is much the same today with its subprefecture, chief town of the district on its borders, in the main, dating from the Ancien Régime. Only ecclesiastically has Bayeux maintained its former status. Before the Revolution the Bishop and his Episcopal Court played a preponderant role in the running of the City and in its architectural and economic development.

A Lay-out dating from Antiquity and the Middle Ages

The lay-out of the City is much marked by the presence of the Gallo-Roman walls that enclosed about a dozen hectares. These fortifications contributed to the City's increasing importance up to the 11th century, and from then onwards came the development of suburbs outside the walls near the various city-gates. This continued further in the 17th century with the establishment of extra-mural religious institutions in these suburbs.

Up to the end of the 17th century the heart of the City remained within its walls dating from Roman times. This basic structure can be divided into three main parts . The first took up all the northern sector within the walls including Rue Saint-Malo and Rue Saint-Jacques that run from east to west.

This is the main artery of the City : the *decumanus maximus* of Gallo-Roman times around which the commercial quarter has grown up with the « Halle aux Viandes » and the streets at right-angles with names evocative of their inhabitants : Rue des Cuisiniers and their activities : Rue Laitière. Beyond the City gates towards Caen, following the artery across the River we come to Rue Saint-Jean around which developed a popular quarter and the City's crafts hence the tanneries and the dyers. There is the « Halle aux Poissons » with halfway down, the « Halle aux Grains ».

In the opposite direction towards Cherbourg is Rue Saint-Patrice, to the north of which, since medieval times is the open space traditionally used for the

Bayeux market.

With one exception these streets from the main artery run southwards. Here on the second axis is the most important section of the City formed by the three streets : Rue des Cuisiniers, Rue du Bienvenu and Rue des Chanoines, the latter leading from the Place au Bois outside the Walls towards Saint-Lô. On this street is the main entrance, the west-door of the Cathedral, around which are the houses of the Cannons. On the northern side of the Cathedral was the Bishop 's Palace (the Hôtel de Ville, today) whilst to the south is the imposing residence of the Dean of the Cathedral Chapter (the Deanery). It stands between two narrow alleys leading to the ramparts. In the Middle Ages, the complex of ecclesiastical buildings extended over the whole south-east quarter of the City bounded by the streets Rue des Chanoines and Rue de la Maîtrise. In the south-west quarter of the City, between Rue Franche, Rue Général-de-Dais and Place Charles-de-Gaulle, stood, until the Revolution, the medieval Castle of Bayeux. The area later became the residential quarter of the notability. A large number of town houses and fine residences of the noblesse or bourgeoisie can still be seen. From the 18th century the City steadily lost its fortifications. For a long time, houses inside the walls were built, up against the ramparts. Later, as the moat was filled in, residences built along the outside were able to use this space as their gardens. To the north of the City, Rue des Bouchers, to the west, Rue Royale and to the south Rue Tardif and Rue de la Poterie. The ramparts form part of the City lay-out and are hardly noticeable though they can be seen in a number of places, notably, « le parking des remparts ». They have disappeared completely from the site of the medieval castle, the demolition of which, began in 1786.

The space cleared was transformed into a pleasant public Square in the first half of the 19th century. Practically nothing remains of the ramparts on the eastern side which leaves the base of the Cathedral in view as well as the whole of the imposing facade of the Episcopal Palace, completely restored at the end of the 18th century.

RUE DE LA MAITRISE

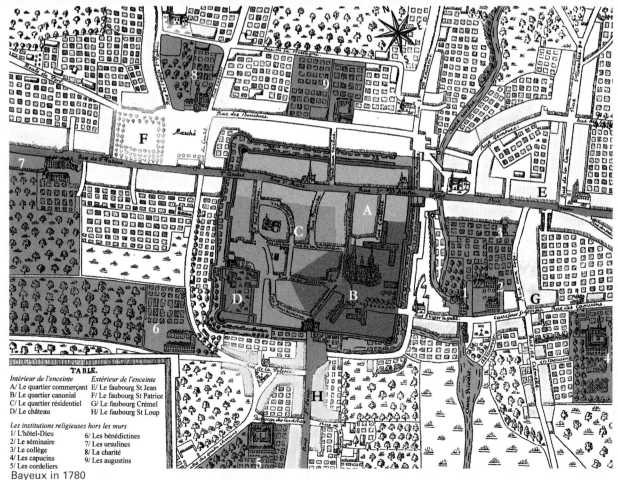

TABLE.

Intérieur de l'enceinte
A/ Le quartier commerçant
B/ Le quartier canonial
C/ Le quartier résidentiel
D/ Le château

Extérieur de l'enceinte
E/ Le faubourg St Jean
F/ Le faubourg St Patrice
G/ Le faubourg Crémel
H/ Le faubourg St Loup

Les institutions religieuses hors les murs
1/ L'hôtel-Dieu
2/ Le séminaire
3/ Le collège
4/ Les capucins
5/ Les cordeliers
6/ Les bénédictines
7/ Les ursulines
8/ La charité
9/ Les augustins

Bayeux in 1780

Thus the City's immediate suburbs known as « faubourgs» just outside each of the City gates, today form an integrate part of the City. So that the old City with its narrow streets could be preserved, having already been spared during the battles following the Landings of June 1944, the Allied Forces built a ring-road to facilitate the passage of men and materials. This not only preserved the heart of historic Bayeux during the conflict but was inordinately useful in the second half of the 20th century as an outer boulevard and subsequently helpful in commercial and industrial development.

An Architectural Heritage Rich and Diverse

Bayeux's medieval heritage suffered greatly in the successive troubles that punctuated the History of Normandy up to the end of the Hundred Years War that ended in a victory for the Forces of the King of France, at the decisive Battle of Formigny in 1450. The City from then on, suffered no major damage.

Thus the rich architectural heritage is linked to the Renaissance and the development of the City in the 15th century. This is noticeable in buildings of fine stone-work in houses for the Cannons of the Cathedral since most houses of the period were more easily and cheaply built of wood and plaster.

Not until the 15th century and the first decades of the 16th was it customary to build dwellings of stone. In the period of intense building towards the end of the Middle Ages numbers of manor houses were built, somewhat stereotyped in character, the staircase in a tower, built on to the facade, some sixty of which can still be found in different parts of Bayeux. Buildings that are very rare are those properly described as Renaissance.

Not until mid-17th century was there any real change in architectural tradition.

This period is known mainly for its new Religious Foundations, marked by the Counter-Reformation.

The Cathedral seen from the banks of the Aure
(Parc Michel-d'Ornano)
▼ Sculpture at no.53 Rue St-Jean

The immediate suburbs (« faubourgs ») were the scene of a great building plan during the episcopate of Monseigneur de Nesmond (1662-1715). A few decades saw the building of the « Hôtel-Dieu » the Seminary and the General Hospital, to the east of the City, to the south were housed, the Capuchin friars and to the west were two new monasteries for the Benedictine and Ursuline Orders. Finally, in the north was built the Convent of the Sisters of Charité-Notre-Dame.

The movement in secular building saw the rise of about ten imposing town-houses still to be seen : rigidly reminiscent of the French classical style.

At the beginning of the 18th century the old part of the City under-went accelerated change when its defences were dismantled. Close to the ancient ramparts, as throughout the City, saw the building of elegant town-houses and complete restoration of the older mansions, the diversity of which demonstrated the tendency of the inhabitants to follow a style of architecture which could easily be restored.

At the outset of the Revolution, the Religious Communities were dissolved, their belongings sold or put in lay hands. With the Concordat of 1801, Bayeux again became the usual seat of a bishop who from that time, extended his authority over both the diocese of Bayeux and Lisieux.

Some Religious Communities came back to their former Houses whilst others such as the Benedictine nuns whose former convent had been taken over as a pocelain factory were forced to go elsewhere, thus participating in an architectural revival that continued throughout the 19th and 20th centuries. Bayeux is not a City firmly fixed in the past where time stands still. A stroll through it shows a harmonious development to the present day.

To search out its heritage means the use of one's eyes and imagination. At each step comes a new discovery : which, at the whim of an inhabitant, an architect or a decorator, an anecdote recalling a great or a small page in the story of those who, over the course of time, formed the face of a city worth living in, in which to spend a few days and to come back to ■

The « Passage des Remparts » at no. 60 Rue Saint-Malo

Rue Franche Maison Gilles Buhot and its tower

Rue Franche no.5 - Hôtel de Rubercy

A courtyard at no. 59 Rue Saint-Martin

no. 17 Rue des Ursulines

In the heart of the Bessin Country that stretches from the Armorican Massif to the Bocage, supreme cattle country and the Parisian Basin to the rich grain-growing plains some ten kilometres from the sea, Bayeux has grown up proportionately on either bank of upper Aure.

The strong links between Bayeux and its rural surroundings, the rich and diverse resources of agriculture are evidence of the produce to be found at the Saturday market in Place Saint-Patrice. Here too until a few decades ago, there was a large market of cattle and pigs (the « cochon de Bayeux »). The old markets in the City centre : « Halles aux viandes, aux poissons », and « au blé » and on the river, the dye works, tanneries and water-mills, all show the extent to which the resources of agriculture and the business derived therefrom, played in the economic activity of the City. Amongst these, should be counted the sea salt industry on the coast near Isigny-sur-Mer, active to the end of the 18th century and the cider-making which took place in the streets of the City. The abundant timber resources at all times, especially in the west of the Bessin (wood from Tronquay, Vernay, and the forestial domain of Cerisy), wood of great importance in carpentry for building. Wood was always indispensible as fuel for the making of ceramics, important for two centuries at Noron-la-Poterie. Wood was also used in the lime-kilns.

Lime was essential for the improvement of the poor quality of the poorer soil of the Bessin. It was used also in the tanneries and in mortar and plaster. The production of lime developed throughout the 18th and 19th centuries as improved furnaces came into use : « le charbon de Littry ».

The chalky subsoil of the region, varying in quality gave character to the City, noticeable in the wood-and-plaster buildings from the Late Middle Ages that remain. The plaster (known as travertin or tuf Calcaire) used on the facades are illustrated : see page 11.

Roof-opening
in varnished ceramics
dating from
the 18th century

Pasture
at Vaux-sur-Aure

Wood and plaster

Fine Jurassic stone from the Creully area was used for the fireplace facings, doorsteps and openings for doors and windows.

Whilst stone came into use in the mid-15th century, buildings entirely of dressed stone were rare ; the Cathedral was the exception. Most stone buildings were of rubble and rough limestone, in differing hues according to their local geological source : greyish-blue from the near upper-tidal levels of Port-en-Bessin, beige and full of tiny fossils, ocre-red from the oolite iron-stone at the base of the Jurassic layer. The latter is seldom visible, having a beige lime skimming from the sandy soils of Saint-Vigor and later from Esquay-sur-Seulles. Typical also of Bayeux and the Bessin country are skimmings encrusted with tiny pebbles, yellowish and brown-ocre, dating from the 18th and early 19th centuries.

Dressed limestone

Limestone was not the only material used in the architectural domain. Today's roofs in slates from the Loire were formerly covered in blue schist from around Balleroy. The streets however, notably around the Cathedral are still paved with red sandstone from May-sur-Orne. Notable too, is the use of ceramics, a traditional craft in the Bessin, rich in good quality clay. The use of brick and tile is sparce and confined largely to glazed ridge-tiles and ceramic dormer facings. In the Middle Ages some floors were paved with ornamental glazed titles from Molay.

Walling of rough limestone

In mentioning the ornamental, the art of stained glass windows and ornamental ironwork is worthy of note. The last-named is seen at its best in balconies and wrought-iron grills, the finest of which date from the 18th century ∎

Limestone plaster on outside walls

« Pebble-dashed » plaster skimming

11

Prehistoric Times

The founding of Augustodurum (old Bayeux) two thousand years ago can be explained only if the lands were, long before the Conquest, densely inhabited, along well defined structured lines. Throughout the oldest phases of pre-history the region underwent profound climatic changes particularly in the different periods of the Ice Age when the sea level declined, leaving a vast plain, joining the British Isles to the Continent. Changes in climate, becoming similar to present-day, came from about 8000 BC onwards and the civilisation of « hunter-gatherers » declined. About BC 6000 the breeding of animals and planting of grain began, by a settled population ; villages became the norm.

The spectacular funeral monuments erected by these first husbandmen between 5000 and 3000 BC are the best testimony we have, to the complexity of the social organisation of the time.
The tumuli of Colombiers-sur-Seulles or Cairon were in the form of mounds, the outer parts being of small limestones, carefully placed, covering one or more collective funeral chambers.
The latter were formed by huge slabs of stone forming a coffin (dolmens) or built entirely of small slabs of limestone and roofed.
The sepulchres were always approached from outside through a long narrow passage through which the dead were carried.

The organisation of the land occupied, centred around the farms, the burial places and a few fortified sites, the importance of which increased in the course of the Bronze and Iron Ages from BC 2000 onwards. Civilisation moved on to the more specific cultivation of land whilst on a European plane there developed an exchange in hard stone, pewter, bronze, gold and amber... These developed at the core of a highly hierarchical society of which the economic activity was essential to its agriculture.

Eperon barré de Castillon (Calvados), an eclosure of 35 hectares, overlooking the Drome Valley ; fortified by the Bajocasses, trees mark the limits of the fortifications

Entering Bayeux, the most impressive pre-historic site is without doubt the fortified camp of Cavalier d'Escures overlooking the valleys of the Aure and the Drôme. An area of five hectares, it consists of a spur with very steep sides, separated from the plateau by a moat, most of which is now filled in, with a rampart some hundred metres long and about ten metres high. Who the occupants were is still unknown but the large number of archeological finds clearly show the stability of human occupation in the area between 2000 and 500 BC. The erection of such fortifications could only have been effected by a People able to group and co-ordinate a workforce of several hundreds in a project differing sharply from everyday needs.

The Camp d'Escures is not the only fortification in the region. There is L'éperon barré de Castillon in the Drôme Valley, about ten kilometres south-east of Bayeux, one of the camps in existence when Julius Caesar conquered Gaul.

Unfortunately, in Caesar's account of the conquest, nothing is mentioned of this region. There is no. mention of the Bajocasse People, whose chief city Augustodurum became, at the beginnings of the 1st century AD. Only in the years following was there mention of this Gaulois People whose links were with the territory and city of which it is capital : the Bessin ■

Polished axe-heads, a knife of silex and the tusk of a wild boar found in a sepulchre at Audrieu (Calvados) circa 4000 BC (Baron Gérard Museum)

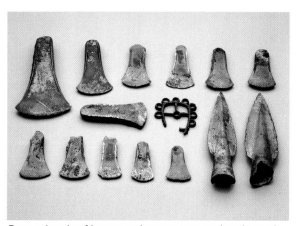

Bronze heads of lances and axes : arms and tools used by inhabitants of the Bessin about 1500 BC found at : Maisons (Calvados)
(Baron Gérard Museum)

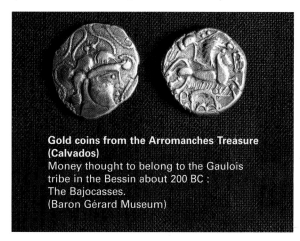

Gold coins from the Arromanches Treasure (Calvados)
Money thought to belong to the Gaulois tribe in the Bessin about 200 BC :
The Bajocasses.
(Baron Gérard Museum)

Situated at the outer-edge of the Roman Empire, what is now Normandy was practically unknown to the geographers and historians of Antiquity. Archeology is an essential source for knowledge of the period that forms a part of our prestigious past. In the course of the second half of the first century BC, the fortified camps (Lat. Oppida), centres of power during independence, were abandoned in favour of the « Romanised » cities, the seats of Imperial administration. Thus it was that Augustodurum, situated about ten kilometres from the Channel, on either side of the river Aure, was chosen. It was at the cross-roads of several important roads, notably the one that joined Noviomagus (Lisieux) to Aulauna (Valognes). The *decumanus maximus* was part of the present Grand Rue that crosses the City from east to west and forming part of the rectangle.

The City developed from the middle of the first century BC along the west bank, the extent of which is still unknown. The central part : walled by the end of the third century, the ramparts of which extend about 400 metres on one side are clearly identifiable still.

The City of antiquity therefore, lies beneath the modern City and reveals its secrets only occasionally in excavation six metres down. The site of the forum, the centre of life in the City has not yet been determined with certainty. It is thought to be in the precints of the Cathedral where, in the 19th century some impressive blocks of sculpture were discovered, part of a vast edifice, considered by some to have been a Roman temple and by others a kind of triumphal arch.

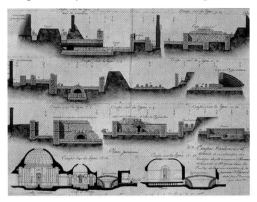

Plan of a thermal complex in Bayeux. Drawn by E. Surville, brother-in-law of Honoré de Balzac (1821)

Remains discovered in other parts of the City, give some idea of the diversity of private dwellings in densely occupied quarters, built in rectangles that determined the ultimate character of the City. The wealthier type of house was of stone, with tiled roofs and with windows sometimes glazed. The humbler dwellings, far more numerous were of wood with walls of mud or clay. There have been a variety of finds in these dwellings (pieces of furniture, pottery, toilet articles...) giving an idea of everyday life in Augustodurum, comparable to that in other cities of Ancient Gaul. The difference is the evidence of military contingents from the Litus Saxonicum (the Saxon shore) confirming the position held by the City from the end of the third century.

As in all Gallo-Roman cities, craftsmanship had an important place in Augustodurum, along with trade, in the economics of the Empire. Oil and wine were transported in amphora but ceramics were used too, imported from across the Channel, from Belgium, the Tarn, and from Central Gaul.

This was on the outskirts of the present City, corresponding to the *suburbium* of that antiquity where the Romanisation was most noteworthy. To the north, near the river (under the present auditorium) about $100m^2$ Roman public baths have been uncovered, consisting of a vast complex in dressed limestone tied in with

Amphora found by fishermen off-shore, Port-en-Bessin (Baron Gérard Museum)

bricks, with a tiled roof. The walls of the interior in the baths and «Stupa» or hot rooms were lined with red and white marble plaques, polished blue stone or painted skimming. The floors, heated from below by hypocausts were paved with polychromed flagstones. The head of Minerva, with a bas-relief of alabaster now preserved in the Baron Gérard Museum is what testifies most to the splendour of this edifice decorated in the Roman tradition of the period and dating from the 2nd century AD.

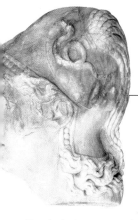

The head of Minerva in alabaster, found in the thermals baths at Augustodurum (Baron Gérard Museum)

Other trades and activities grew up around the City. A lime Kiln dating from the end of the 2nd century on the road-side to Aulauna (now Rue Saint-Patrice), 3.5 metres in height still remains. An exciting discovery in the same area was some painted plaster, making it possible to restore what had been the home of a wealthy person in the *suburbium* of Augustodurum. The necropolises were also outside the City. The one which has yielded the richest sepulchres (sarcophagi, bronze ornaments, glass vases...) was discovered on the east bank of the Aure, on the sides of Mount Phaunus, overlooking the north-east side of the City, (Rue de la Cavée). Mount Phaunus is symbolic of the rise of Christianity in the City. It is thought to have been the scene of the martyrdom of Saint Floxel, under Maximin I about 235-238. Here also were the first acts of evangelism by Saint Exupery at the end of the 4th century and finally the celebrated teaching of one of his glorious successors : Saint Vigor (6th Bishop of Bayeux) and founder of a monastery that overlooks the ancient necropolis. His episcopal throne of red marble, a sculpture dating, according to tradition from about 511 is in the Parish Church dedicated to him.

At the end of the 4th century when its people became Christian, Bayeux took on a religious dimension as the seat of a bishop. After the Empire collapsed in the middle of the 5th century, first under the Merovingian then the Carolingian dynasties, the Bessin became part of Neustria. The authority of the Roman Prefects was assumed by the Counts. The power of the bishops in temporal matters in their dioceses however, was marked.

Hugh, Bishop of Bayeux in the 7th century was not only from the Gallo-Roman aristocracy but from the royal line, being the nephew of Charles Martel. The influence of Bishops of Bayeux at this time was considerable, as much in temporal matters as in spiritual. In the latter their lives were such that many were canonised (between the 4th and the 9th centuries at least nine Bayeux bishops became saints). They are found in the iconographies of the Bayeux parish churches, and in the Bessin and in those of the Cathedral ■

Ornaments dating from the 4th century found in the Necropolis of Pouligny (Baron Gérard Museum)

Saint Exupery and the Druid of Mount Phaunus by Nicolas Vergnaux (Baron Gérard Museum)

The Bayeux Tapestry

The Viking Heritage of William the Conqueror

The violence of the destruction caused by the Vikings, Danish and Norwegian pirates who plundered the Neustrian coasts from the first decades of the 9th century was an overwhelming disaster for almost a century, the countryside was devastated, commerce collapsed, churches, monasteries and libraries and the scriptoria in them were ruined and dispersed. Thus the remains of the Bishops of Bayeux who were saints left the Diocese.

In 858 Bayeux was sacked ; the Scandinavians pillaged the Cathedral treasures, stole the shrine of Saint Regnobert and murdered Bishop Baltfrid. Tradition has it that Rollo, the Viking chief ravaged Bayeux in 891, killing Count Beranger and carrying off his daughter, the lovely Popée, made her his concubine and thus assured his claim to the Duchy.

It was to attempt to end this state of affairs that Charles the Simple decided in 911 to give to Rollo (or Rolf) authority over the Lower Seine Valley, provided he defend it against other Vikings, that he be baptized, and be faithful to the King. In 924 King Raoul ceded to Rollo Le Mans and Bayeux. Thus, the Bessin and its capital were again an integral part of the Duchy of Normandy. Although the presence of Scandinavian troops in the Bessin responded little, to Ducal authority before the middle of the 10th century, Bayeux could well be considered as the secondary capital of the Province. The Dukes coinage was minted there in Carolingian fashion and they usually resided there. The young Richard I was sent there to learn Danish.

At the beginning of the 11th century prosperity began to return. The Bessin monasteries, like Cerisy Abbey slowly put ruin behind them. Bayeux Cathedral looked for relics to replace those lost ; it had a vast programme of restoration too. Normandy was recognised by Rome as known to be favourable to ecclesiastical reform. In the second half of the 11th century, Duke William's reign was marked by the creation of the Anglo-Norman Kingdom ; thus the Duchy rose in importance and the City of Bayeux reached its zenith.

Plaque commemorating Bayeux's homage to Popée Berenger, daughter of the Count of Bessin on her return to the City as wife of Rollo, founder of the Duchy of Normandy. Commorative plaque on the façade of the Hôtel de Ville.

The Principal Characters in the Conquest

The central figure in the conquest of England is William of course, (1027-1087) eighth Duke of Normandy, natural son of Robert the Magnificient who died in Nicea (Turkey) on a pilgrimage to the Holy Land in 1035.

William's adolescence was marked by a long period of unrest. The young duke managed nevertheless to impose himself on and assume the support of his vassals. Although he himself was vassal to the King of France his own authority made him as a sovereign independent. In order to assert his position, he placed his relatives in places of temporal or spiritual authority in the Duchy. Thus, the main characters in the Conquest of England were William's half-brothers at his side : Robert Count of Mortain and Odo (Eudes) of Conteville to whom he had given the Episcopal seat of Bayeux about 1050 (he was then only 13 or 14 years old). Odo and Robert were, after their brother's accession to the throne, in possession of the most lands of all the Norman Lords in England.

In passing, it should be said that Odo, as Bishop of Bayeux should be considered one of the most noteworthy of his time. He played an important part in the re-organisation : administrative, intellectual and spiri-

tual of the Church.

At the same time Odo improved greatly the standing of the Cathedral and its Clergy by his largess. He was a prelate who, after the Conquest, assumed the title : Count of Kent and concerned himself with temporal affairs. In England in the King's absence, his position was that of Regent, notably between 1076 and 1080. Unfortunately, his political blunders and his ambitions led his brother to imprison him in the castle keep at Rouen in 1082.

Set free on the King's death, he took sides in the dispute over the succession between his nephews. Exiled from England in 1088, he returned to Bayeux deprived of his title of Count and shorn of his English possessions. Indefatigable man of action, we next find Odo, with Pope Urban II preaching the Crusade in 1095. Charged by the Sovereign Pontif, with the Norman contingent, he left for the Holy Land in September 1096, but never arrived there. Wintering in Sicily with Count Roger, he died at Palmero in January 1097. In homage to his ecclesiastical rank and royal ties he was buried in the Cathedral there.

The Scandinavian origin of the Norman dukes during the 11th century added to their interests in the complex diplomatic and military contest that took place between the states that grew out of the Viking movement and the kingdoms of the North Sea.

England was in the forefront during the first decades of the century with fresh Danish invasions. The King, Ethelred II (the « Unready ») husband of Emma daughter of Duke Richard I of Normandy ; lost his throne in 1013 to the Danes.

He and his family fled to Normandy, including young Edward whose uncle, Duke Richard took care of him. In 1042, on the death of the last Danish King, Hardicanute, Edward succeeded to the Throne, known as Edward the Confessor. Under the influence of Godwin, the powerful Count of Wessex, he married one of his daughters : Edith, sister of Harold Godwinson and Tostig, brother-in-law of Matilda, daughter of Count Baldwin of Flanders, whom William of Normandy married in 1051.

Edward

Harold

William

Odo

The Bayeux Tapestry

The Tapestry : a story with a moral of Norman Times

The Tapestry of Bayeux, that tells of William of Normandy's succession to the English throne is not merely a narrative of military prowess. It is also and perhaps primarily, a work destined to edify spiritually the faithful who worshipped in Bayeux Cathedral. Harold had sworn an oath of fidelity over sacred relics to William, Most Christian Duke of Normandy. He had had himself crowned King of England, in William's place. Punishment for this act of perjury was terrible ; he died during the dreadful Battle of Hastings, ending the battle that Duke William felt compelled to fight to gain the throne of which he had been deprived. The moral issue is at the heart of the story. There is no. doubt that the Tapestry was made in a monastery in South-east England on the orders of the Bishop of Bayeux, and as its style shows, ressembling the illuminated Norman manuscripts of the period found on that side of the Channel.

The Tapestry is in fact an embroidery in wool of eight different colours, on eight lengths of unbleached linen stitched firmly together. The narrative unfolds along the linen 50 cms wide and some 70 metres long. It is a wall-hanging intended for the nave of Bayeux Cathedral, for use every July on the Feast of the Relics. It was probably displayed for the first time on 14th July 1077, in the presence of the King and Queen at the dedication of the new Cathedral, built by Odo. It remained in the midst of the Cathedral treasures until the Revolution when it passed into lay hands and was exhibited to the public, recognised for its exceptional artistic and historic value as a chef d'œuvre of Norman art.

An exceptional document

The story related in the Bayeux Tapestry, is told in a sequence of scenes, each with a brief Latin text. The scenes are divided with environmental skill by pieces of architecture or foliage which, by the quality of the artistry does not detract from either the unity or style of the whole. The flow of events builds up to the main action. This is framed above and below by a frieze, people with beasts and birds (cocks, peacecocks, rams, stags, bears, fishes, lions and camels...), mythological monsters (centaurs, dragons and fabulous birds) but also lone figures, scenes from everyday life, and illustrations of fables with a moral, by Aesop or Phedre (The Fox and the Crow, The Lamb and the Wolf, The Hound and her Pups, The Crane and the Wolf, and The Lion and its Cubs).

The rich variety of illustrations are worthy of note, comprising : more than five hundred people, over two hundred dogs, about thirty buildings, and some forty ships. The Bayeux Tapestry is also a mine of information in which every aspect of life in the 11th century is described in detail. Various differences make it possible to distinguish between the opposing sides : like Harold, the English have moustaches, whilst the Normans have their heads shaved backand sides. Those in the Court circle can be identified by their symbols of power (Clothing, accessories and attitudes). Important people are recognisable in the crowd, including the main protagonists who in peacetime are on horseback, unarmed, with their pack of hounds, falcon on wrist, or dine at table using knives, wine-cups, bowls, plates and drinking-horns. Within the palace, Counts, Duke and King wear their robes of State, enthroned in majesty, the seats richly decorated, and cushions provided. Those of high military rank, have also an important place. Arms of the combatants are shown in minute detail (axes, clubs, lances, swords, bows and arrows, shields, helmets coats of mail and standards...) harness and saddlery. Ships are portrayed, not only with their armament and methods of propulsion but show also the strategy and tactics in warfare.

The Bayeux Tapestry

The Clergy play a minor role but the Tapestry gives a wealth of religious detail : Church furnishings, clerical hair-cuts and tonsures, sacred vestments, also the role of the prelates in the arrangement of ceremonies, whether nuptial, funeral or sacramental.

In second place but not forgotten are many aspects of daily life, the ploughmen, the carpenters or labourers using their tools. Too, there are the cooks with a complete set of ustensils preparing roasts or stews from pork beef or mutton, fish or fowl, all of which is washed down with wine.

The events described in the Tapestry and the historical sources from which confirm them

Above the frieze of the Tapestry are a series of numbers, written in ink, put there in the 19th century, so that the scenes may be followed chronologically.
The events cover a period of three years from 1064 to

1066 inclusive. The period can be divided into three phases, though not of equal importance : Harold's visit to Normandy 1064-1065 (Scenes 1-23) ; the death of Edward the Confessor on 5th January 1066 and the preparation for the Norman invasion during the Spring and Summer of 1066 (24-38) and finally the landing in England (28th September 1066) followed by the Battle of Hastings (14th October) (scenes 39-58). Study of the scenes in this order corresponds to historical accounts of the time, still extant « The Gesta » (heroic exploits) by Guillaume de Poitiers and Guillaume de Jumièges, (written about 1070-1075) and completed at the beginning of the 12th century with

interpolations by Orderic Vital and Robert de Torigni and then about 1160 by « Le roman de Rou », the work of Wace, a Canon of Bayeux Cathedral.

In 1064, Edward the Confessor of England entrusted his brother-in-law, the Count of Wessex Harold Godwinson, leader of the Anglo-Saxon party in succession to the Throne, to make known to his cousin William of Normandy, his decision : having no descendant that he had chosen him as heir (1-6).

Harold, instead of landing on the Norman coast, was blown off course, and landed on the banks of the Somme, in the lands of Guy de Ponthieu. Held in the Château of Beaurain (near Abbeville), the Duke of Normandy had to pay a ransom to free him. (7-13).

Once freed, Harold is made welcome in Normandy. The Duke invites him to take part in a military expedition against Conan, Count of Brittany. Crossing the Bay at Mont-Saint-Michel the troops besiege Dol, advance to Rennes, then Dinan where the Count of Brittany is forced to hand the keys of the Town to William. On the battlefield, the victorious Duke of Normandy knighted Harold. In homage to his gallantry he made him a knight of Normandy (14-21).

Finally before returning to England the Count of Wessex swore fidelity to the Duke of Normandy over the Cathedral relics (22-24).

On his return Harold met the old King who, worn out by ill-health, died on 5th January 1066. He was buried in Westminster Abbey which had only been consecrated a few weeks earlier. The day after the funeral, the

Assembly of Notables decided to offer the crown to Harold who accepted it in spite of his oath. Soon however an ill omen appeared in the sky : a strange moving star with a twinkling streak. It was Halley's Comet, visible for a whole week from 24th April to 1st May 1066 (25-33).

The Duke of Normandy sought the advice of Odo, his half-brother. It was he who suggested assembling a fleet to invade England. The fleet was ready by mid-August but the crossing was delayed until 27th September. In the course of that night, almost 400 ships put to sea, with 15 000 men and 2 000 horses aboard. Amongst the ships that sailed was the «Mora», the Duke's ship, flying a pennant at the mast-head blessed by the Pope (34-38).

The following morning the fleet reached Pevensey and the Force took off for Hastings, where the Normans took up positions.

Harold's troops had just pulled off a bloody victory near York against the Norwegians under Tostig, the King's own brother. Harold then forced-marched his troops to Hastings. On the morning of 14th October 1066 the decisive battle took place. William with his baton of command urged on his troops. The archers took up their positions and the horsemen galloped forward in a long ride, then were held up by a wall of shields that protected the English infantry. During the fighting the King's brothers Lewine and Guyrd were killed. The dead were so numerous that they are shown on the lower frieze of the Tapestry.

Advancing, the heavy Norman cavalry began to founder at the foot of a hill, protected by surrounding swamp in which stakes had been driven with the tops

sharply pointed. The English had regrouped behind these defences. The Normans fell back in disorder. The issue of the Battle was now in question. To reassure his men, Duke William took off his helmet. The Normans then took courage and launched a decisive assault. In spite of the protection afforded by troops of his elite, Harold was mortally wounded by an arrow in his right eye and the retreat of the English troops became a veritable route. (48-58).

Thus was the brutal ending on the Tapestry on the evening of 14th October 1066. The linen with the rest of the epic, time has destroyed but it is easy to imagine it, with the Coronation of William in Westminster Abbey on 25th December 1066 ■

The Cathedral

In the first place, Bayeux Cathedral appears to be an edifice in Gothic style of the 13th-15th centuries. But scarcely has one passed beneath the west facade when one realises that this is a Norman church of the 11th-12th centuries with a gothic exterior.

We are within the Cathedral which Bishop Hugh d'Ivry, nephew of Duke Richard I, predecessor of Odo of Conteville, deemed worthy of the relics of Saint Rasiphe and Saint Raven, martyrs, Saxon in origin, whose bodies were discovered in the parish churchyard of Saint-Vaast-sur-Seulles, about twenty kilometres south of Bayeux.

This is important on several counts. During the 8th and 9th centuries, the relics of the Holy Bishops of Bayeux like the remains of Saint Exupere, Saint Vigor or Saint Regnobert left the Diocese to save them from destruction by the Vikings. They never came back to Bayeux. That there were others worthy to « take their place » is one of the best proofs of a real revival in the Cathedral City of the 11th Century, from a spiritual as well as a socio-economic viewpoint.

Their presence certainly influenced the architectural scheme put in place. The oldest part of the Norman Cathedral is its crypt, built beneath the Choir and destined to hold the precious remains of the saints and the Cathedral treasure, placed around them. One proof of the awe in which the relics were held, is that in 1065 Harold's oath was made in their presence.

Bishop Odo, in making Harold's oath a central part of events on the Tapestry, knew well how to heighten the dimension of mystique.

The Cathedral Odo consecrated in the presence of William and Matilda on 14th July 1077, a « chef d' œuvre » in primitive Norman Architecture was set on fire in 1105 when Henry I « Beauclerc » besieged the City. The work of restoration undertaken over decades was Anglo-Norman in type, but was transformed by the end of the 12th century into a vast programme of renovation in the style of Gothic borrowed from Ile de France. This was not finished until a century later and was finally completed during the 14th and 15th centuries by other additions and embellishments. The Cathedral comes down to us in its composite form and so one sees the remarkable evolution of Medieval Norman Religious architecture.

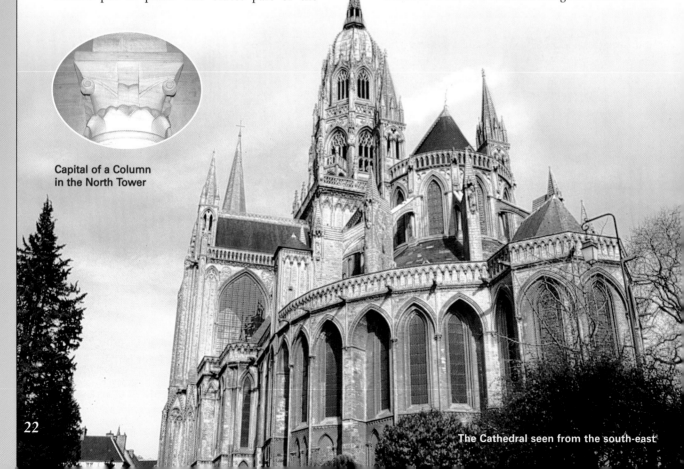

Capital of a Column in the North Tower

The Cathedral seen from the south-east

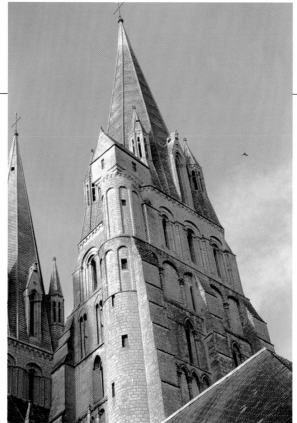
The North Tower

The vestiges
of the early Norman Cathedral

In the middle of the 11th century the complete rebuilding of the first Cathedral Church that dated from Carolingian times, was under the impetus of Bishop Odo. Completed in less than fifty years, thanks to the considerable revenues of the Diocese, the remaining parts dating from that period, give an idea of the extent of the work.

In entering the Cathedral beneath the twin towers we find ourselves in a Norman cathedral of the 11th century. The towers were built in the years 1070-1090. The architectural techniques, solid and powerful with the somewhat stark decoration of the supporting columns, are striking. Notable is the vaulting at ground-level of the South Tower in cradle form with a supporting arch. The North Tower's vaulting is almost hemispherical, reinforced by the supporting arches, crossing perpendicularly. One wonders at the work of Norman architects in their research on pointed arches. Originally these formed part of a covered gallery supported by columns, giving on to another gallery inside the nave. The latter was taken away in the second half

of the 13th century but finally replaced in 1775 by a gallery for the Cathedral Organ.

The second major part of the 11th century cathedral is the Crypt, now entered by a modern stairway in the north ambulatory. Its size is equivalent to three bays between arches, of the Gothic Choir. The Crypt has a triple nave, the arches of which are supported by pillars, surmounted by capitals, typical of primitive Norman architecture (c. 1050-1060). One pillar only, the last on the right, is different ; it has a godroon style capital of the 12th century) ; opposite, on the far wall, there is an opening made recently, making it possible to see the remains of the 12th century wall of the Carolingian Cathedral. As to other sculptured stonework, most of it dates from the 15th century, at the time when the crypt was rediscovered after a century of neglect. So too, on the right, the tomb of Jean de Boissey buried in 1412 and on his left lies the mutilated figure of Canon Gervais de Larchamp and above him a painting of Hell with the dead man being presented to the Virgin, this, as with the other murals and the eighteen Angel musicians, all are painted on the vault ceiling.

The 11th Century Crypt

Finally, of special note are two half-pillars with very large capitals. These came from the 11th century transept-crossing, in the decades : 1060-1070. The sculpture on the capital near the tomb of Jean de Boissey is of God the Father in great glory, with two seraphim at his side and a small child on his knees, giving his blessing. The other capital, on a pillar near the opposite wall has a sculpture of Christ with Saint Peter on his left and Saint Thomas on his right. These are the two most important Norman capitals of William the Conqueror's time, known to us.

The Cathedral

Cannon Gervais de Larchamp (15th century)

The Gothic Cathedral

The episcopate of Henry (1165-1205), former Dean of Salisbury contemporary of Thomas a Becket, Archbishop of Caterbury and King Henry II Plantagenet, marked a decisive turning point in the evolution of the architecture of Bayeux Cathedral. The Prelate who saw Normandy re-attached to the Franch Crown oriendated the character of the edifice in that direction away from the Norman-Anglo-Norman culture. Work on the Gothic Cathedral that he had begun would not be finished until a century later, after having affected in turn different parts of the Building.

The Ile-de-France architects were to put in place gothic arches that were joined by ribs to the vaulting. The ribs were then directed downwards to join with vertical supports, reinforced externally by supporting arches, reduced to a minimum, outward pressure on the walls. The latter were to have large openings to accommodate stained-glass windows. Due to this, in the closing decades of the 12th century the lower sides of the nave were strengthened. A century later, parts of the walls were taken down to give access to side-chapels built between the end of the 13th and the middle of the 14th century. In the same building programme saw the appearance of the Chapter House adjoining the North Tower. Built in the 14th century, it has retained its medieval enamelled paving on which a labyrith has been drawn, known as the Jerusalem pathway. A large mural dominates the building dating from the first quarter of the 15th century in which the Virgin is depicted surrounded by members of the Chapter.

Influenced from the first by their counterparts in the Ile-de-France the Norman architects set out to make use of the same methods to produce in Bayeux a style reminiscent of 13th century Gothic, though distinctly regional, the Choir of Bayeux Cathedral is an outstanding example.

The edifice was 80 metres in length. We know this because the transept was in its present position in Norman times and at the point of crossing were galleries that extended from the nave into the chancel and above the choir-stalls. Both the nave and transept had an ordinary wooden ceiling at about 22 metres from the floor. After the fire of 1105, the building was completely restored and refitted ; probably between 1120 and 1130, the lower parts of the nave were completed, except the last bay, (finally restored in the 19th century). On the quadrilateral pillars of the 11th century (transformed into Gothic) were deployed the wide vaulted arches with crenelated decoration, chevrons, lozanges and fantastic masques, above which, the wall-face was covered with geometrical designs, in Anglo-Norman style. In the niches were placed bas-reliefs (the juggler and his monkey ; a bishop giving his blessing, a bird of prey with a head in its claws, over a lion ; another bishop, fingers raised in blessing ; a bearded man, naked standing on a head, monsters inter-laced ; a dragon surmonted by a griffin). The sculptures are reminiscent of the illuminated manuscripts from English scriptoria of the time, particularly in Canterbury, with more than a trace of Scandinavian influence, as in Bayeux. The lower parts of the nave in Bayeux Cathedral are striking evidence that the City and its clergy as a powerful political and cultural entity, was part of a civilisation to be found on both sides of the Channel.

The Norman Choir was dismantled to make way for the one we have now, put in place circa 1230-1245. Consisting of four sections of vaulting of arches in a semi-circle it is surrounded by an ambulatory that opens on the chapels that radiate from it. It is on three elevations the main level being central (the triforium) is walled in on either side which excludes light from the windows. There is something in its ample proportions which recalls the ancient Roman tribunes.

windows and on the other of putting in the fine new woodwork. The stalls were made by J. Lefèvre (1589) of Caen, a sculpter and cabinet-maker. This was the major element of change, followed later by the High Altar in gray marble consecrated in 1771. The Cross and Chandeliers were ordered from the silver-smith, P. Caffieri (1714-1774). The decoration of the fluting on the columns behind the High Altar and the wrought-iron grills date from this period.

The Choir Vaulting (13th century)

The interior of the Cathedral in the 19th century lithograph by A. Maugendre

Amongst other peculiarities of its Norman style is the geometric austerity, underlined by the accentuated mouldings and the profusion of its columns. Also characteristic is the extent of repetitive decoration based on trefoil, quadrilobes and polylobe medallions, with foliage, fantastic beasts and a few animated scenes. On the vaulting too, is an ensemble of painted medallions and effigies of the first Bishop-Saints of Bayeux.

The major changes in the Gothic choir, consisted on the one hand of taking down the medieval leaded glass

Arts treasures kept in the lower room of the treasury : paintings from the 13th and 14th centuries and sculpture from the 15th

The Cathedral

To return to architectural changes in Gothic : about 1245-1255, the higher parts of the Nave were altered. The work was a somewhat daring venture since it consisted of taking away the triforium and giving prominence to the large windows. The contrast between the light of the Nave and the sudued light of the Choir is in large part due to these windows, that form a sort of glass cage. Until 1760, the stone-work was decorated and there were statues of the Bishop Saints of Bayeux. We cannot leave this section without noting the imposing character of the pulpit with its carving depicting : The Triumph of Faith in the world. The work was carried out by the sculpter J.-L. Mangin.

The last great phase of the work in Gothic architecture was between 1260 and 1280 (before work began on the Central Tower) and concerns the Transept. Its two arms were decorated in the same fashion though there are differences of style at the lower level where blind arcades were added. Each has a stained-glass window, restored in the 19th century. In the North Transept, notice the niches in the balustrade at the base of the window with figures of the Apostles from the 12th century that have been used again, as also have 14th century murals, heavily restored, consecrated to the life of Saint Nicolas and Saint Thomas Becket. In the South Transept that leads to the Sacristy there is a large reredos put there in the middle of the 18th century. It hides the entrance to an ancient chapel, that now forms part of the space where the Cathedral Treasure is kept.

The Cathedral Treasure has been, since the 13th century, kept on the first floor in a small building in the North Ambulatory, facing the entrance to the Crypt. The ground-floor, recently refitted, houses some murals of the 13th and 14th century and a number of mutilated medieval statues. Protestant troops damaged them in 1562-1563. The 11th century treasure,

The Cathedral Exterior

amassed due to the generosity of Bishop Odo and King William, was sadly taken elsewhere during the troubles. Fortunately there are on the first floor some exhibits of exceptional splendour : an ivory casket in silver and gilt, of Arab origin (10th-11th century), a silk chasuble (12th century) said to have belonded to Saint Regnobert, an impressive cabinet (13th century) intended for reliquaries and sacred vessels, an unusual episcopal folding seat in wrought iron (14th century) and lastly the 15th century cabinet in which, formerly the Tapestry was kept.

The Cathedral exterior

The two six-floor towers that form the western arcade of the building still retain their Norman openings and blind arcades with semi-circular arches dating from the first half of the 12th century. The towers, originally with roofs, were, in the 13th century, enhanced with stately stone spires that had to be strengthened with robust counterforts and consolidated stone-facings. The latter were then given further ormentation with blind gothic arches.

The Cathedral West Door gives the impression of a decorative veneer to the building. Made up of five arches, two of which are blind bays, the three others being portals dating from the very end of the 13th century. The central doorway, damaged unfortunately, at the end of the 18th century has a tympan, devoted to the Life of the Virgin. The door on the left still has sculpture devoted to Christ's Passion, from the Washing of Feet, low-left up to The Crucifixion. It is surmonted, finally by a scene, mutilated unfortunately, of Christ in majesty.

On the right-hand doorway, the sculpture above, depicts scenes from the Last Judgement. On the lowest level are the Damned, awaited by the Devil at the gates of Hell ; above that, is the Resurrection of the Dead. Above, the third level, the Elect enter Paradise. Christ seated in Judgement, presides in majesty over the whole.

Above the main doorway are a series of medallions in the centre of each is someone at prayer; this is very probably the figure of a donor to the Cathedral, having contributed to the embellishment of the edifice.

The section above consists of a large window devoted to the Life of the Virgin, covered inside the Cathedral by the organ woodwork. Finally, below the gable, the facade is surmounted by a gallery with ten statues, effigies of the Bishop-Saints of Bayeux.

The portal of the South Transept too, retains its original sculpture, from the end of the 13th century. Above the two trilobate doors is a tympan on three levels, devoted to the life of an Anglo-Norman saint, Thomas a Becket, who lived a century before.

The first section alludes to the conflicts and attempts at reconciliation between the King of England Henry II Plantagenet and his Archbishop. The second section

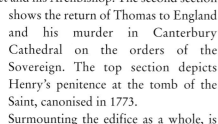

shows the return of Thomas to England and his murder in Canterbury Cathedral on the orders of the Sovereign. The top section depicts Henry's penitence at the tomb of the Saint, canonised in 1773.

Surmounting the edifice as a whole, is the Transept dating from the 14th century from which rises, at two levels the central tower, to a height of over 80 metres. The higher section of the tower with its bronze summit added in the 19th century, but in the Flamboyant style of the lower tower, built after the end of the Hundred Years War, between 1477 and 1479 on the initiative od Bishop Louis d'Harcourt, Patriarch of Jerusalem. Among the rich ornamentation on the lower tower, are the Arms of the Prelate with Archiepiscopal Cross, alternating with the Fleur de Lys on a shield, surmounted by the Royal Crown ∎

The South Doorway consecrated to Thomas a Becket

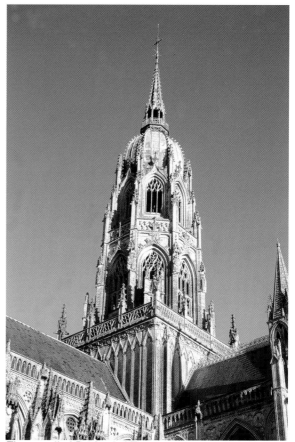

The so-called Patriarchal Tower

Episcopal Palace

The former palace of the Bishops of Bayeux, built on the north side of the cathedral is built around what became, Place de la Liberté and its two-hundred-year-old Plane-tree.

Today, the usual entrance is from the west facade of the Cathedral, taking the passage at the end of the Chapter House. This passage is named after Engineer Flachat to whom we owe the work of stabilising the supports of the Central Tower and thus ensuring its safety.

Window of the former archives-room of the Chapter

On the esplanade dominated by the steps leading to the Palace inner-courtyard, there was in former times the ancient archives-room of the Chapter. All that remains of this medieval building is a window composed of a rounded arch ornamented with geometric designs that has been moved to the level of the steps and is in the wall of a private house.

At the foot of the esplanade is the Chapter Library built in the middle of the 15th century, which, on the first floor has an amazing neogothic interior of the first half of the 19th century.

The Chapter Library

The Palace was, until the end of the 19th century joined on to the Cathedral by a wing that communicated with the North Transept, the site of the present Sacristy, also built in Neogothic style in 1900. Beyond this there is the oldest part of the residence (west wing), that replaced, without a shadow of doubt the residence of Bishop Odo. The Building, several times

The oldest part of the Palace

rebuilt since the 11th century retains its character, typically that of the end of the Middle Ages.

From that period dates the main entrance and the decoration on the higher sections of the facade ; unfortunately the windows were damaged somewhat in the 18th century. The vaulted rooms on the ground floor were formerly used to store the confidential papers of the ecclesiastical couts. The entrance to the ecclesiastical prison in the opposite facade was through a somewhat elegant door, decorated in the Flamboyant style, leading to an inner courtyard (Jardin Saint-Yves) in which there are the remains of a twelfth-century cloister.

The upper floor appears to have been the residential part of the Palace up to the final third of the 18th century, as shown by the magnificent Regency style panelling still to be found in the central section. The North Wing at the end of which was the main entrance to the Palace formed the official part of the residence. The former main entrance leads to the Grand Staircase (dating from the last third of the 18th century) with a magnificent balustrade in wrought iron that includes the arms of Monsignor Pierre-Jules-Caesar de Rochechouart. It leads to an ante-room

The Arms of Monsig de Rochechouart

leading in turn to the Audience Chamber of the Bishop. The most remarkable thing about this state-room is the ceiling. It is of oak panelling with intricate triangular designs within each panel. It is in this room that Seguier, Royal Chancellor, arrived in 1640, in the name of the King, Louis XIII to repress the Popular Rising against royal power, better known by the name of The bare-footed revolt.

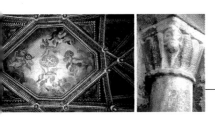

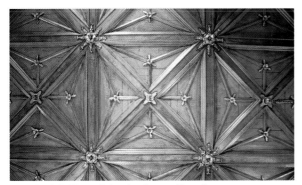

Panelled Ceiling of the Audience Chamber

The Wing now used by the Police Department

The real jewel of the Episcopal Palace is the Bishop's private Chapel situated at the end of the Audience Chamber. It was probably installed in an ancient tower in the city-ramparts and juts out the other side of the wall. The interior furnishing was carried out in the episcopate of Louis de Canossa (1516-1531) and is one of the finest architectural achievements of the French Renaissance that has survived in Lower Normandy.

The decorative sequence, damaged by Protestant troops in 1562 and 1563 was redone in a masterly fashion in the first half of the 17th century, with an impressive ensemble of 52 murals in the form of a celestial concert consisting of Angel musicians and Cherubim.

The wing enclosing the Palace courtyard on the eastern side is austere and was only built in the second quarter of the 19th century was designed to accomodate the Police Headquarters and its prisons.

In fact, when Monsignor de Cheylus was exiled to Jersey in 1791 the Palace became the seat of civil authority : housing the Hôtel de Ville, the Sous-prefecture and the Law-court. This explains why the Inner-courtyard was chosen for the Plane tree, now two-hundred years old : L'Arbre de la Liberté, planted on 30th March 1797.

Finally, we cannot leave the Episcopal Palace without mention of the aggrandissement between 1770 and 1771 by Monsignor Pierre-Jules-Caesar de Rochecouart. From the plans of the architect Leblond rose a vast edifice designed as an eminent residence.

This imposing Pile is, along Rue Laitière, at the far end of the grounds. To the north of the medieval palace were the former Episcopal Gardens, which became the Esplanade of l'Hôtel de Ville overlooked by the main facade of the complex ■

Gravure The facade of the Palace, erected by Monsignor de Rochechouart (taken from Rue Larcher) (the present Hôtel de Ville)

The Deanery

A residence built by Dean Néel de Cristot

On the South Front of the Cathedral, set back slightly, behind a large doorway, is the former residence of the Dean of the Cathedral Chapter. With the Bishop's Palace and the Sanctuary we find a group of episcopal buildings that have stood the test of time.

The Dean of the Chapter is the second most important person after the Bishop in the Diocese. As head of the Chapter : a body of Cathedral Clergy given the titles of canons, the Chapter forms the Bishop's Council and acts as his deputy when the Episcopal See is vacant.

In medieval times, the Canons' revenues were large and came from Cathedral Patrimony (richly endowed with lands under the episcopate of Odo and in the reign of William). The Cathedral revenues were divided into as many parts (Prebends) as there are charges on the Chapter (composed of foty-eight titular members). Naturally the size of these prebends varied according to the place in the hierarchy of each Canon (Dean, Sub-dean, Precentor, Sub-precentor, Treasurer...)

Inscription from the house of a canon no.1 Impasse Glatigny

All of these properties and notably the residences of the Canons, forming a Canonial Quarter (comprising the Streets : Lambert-Forestier, Des Chanoines and de la Maîtrise) were sold as National Property, during the Revolution.

In Cathedral ceremonial, members of the Chapter, have of course a place of importance, notably by the choir-stalls reserved for them. The door in the South Transept with the title of «Dean's Door» indicates the somewhat privileged position of this high dignitary. Formerly, only the Grand Dean was privileged to cross this threshold, though only on two occasions : on his solemn entry, following his election and later : on the occasion of this funeral.

The site of the Deanery was, from the 11th century onwards, the residence of the Treasurer of the Chapter until the 13th century when it became the Deanery,

having been rebuilt on numerous occasions. The present building dates from the first half of the 18th century, built by Dean Louis François Neel de Cristot (1735-1740) before he was appointed Bishop of Sées by King Louis XV. The imposing gate-way opening on to the street, erected by Dean Charles de Longaunay de Franqueville (1655-1697) dates from the century before. It consists of a massive arch, solidly built of dressed stone in relief, crowned by a cornice supporting a balustrade, ornamented by a seies of «pots-à-feu».

The external frontal bears the Arms of Monsignor Nicolas-Pierre Didiot (1856-1866) Bishop of Bayeux, who also had work done to ensure the safety of the Cathedral central tower. These Arms are a reminder that the property (belonging to the Department of Calvados) was the Episcopal Residence from 1802 to 1906.

The site on which the Deanery stood testifies to the prestige of the occupant. It is in the heart of the Medieval City. To be noted too is the garden, now a public park. Behind the building it becomes the main courtyard of the Cathedral. The whole amounts to a perfect example of how the people of Bayeux benefitted by the demolition of the ramparts. Before that they were very much «closed in». With the walls gone and the moat filled in, the garden was extended to Rue Tardif which formerly ran round the other side of the City walls.

On the ground-floor of the interior of the building there remains something of the ecclesistical of the episcopal residence that it was all through the 19th century. It is interesting to note that the bishops of Bayeux tended to restore here, in the years 1820-1830, the grandeur of their ancient palace. There is an Audience Chamber of the Restoration period, furnished with an astonishing gallery of portraits consisting of all the prelates who succeeded to the bishopric of Bayeux from the 4th century onwards. Ninety-two in all, the earliest of the portraits were painted in the 17th century and hung in the Audience Chamber of the original palace.

Entrance gateway erected by Dean de Longaunay

Attached to the length of the building is the Episcopal Chapel, put in place during the episcopate of Monsignor François Robin (1836-1855). Within these precincts, and more particularly in the tiny bureau alongside the room known as the «Salle des Evèques» young Thérèse Martin (Sainte Thérèse de Lisieux) came, on 31st October 1887, to plead with Monsignor Flavien Hugonin (1867-1898), for the necessary dispensation to enter the Carmel, despite her tender age (she was not yet fourteen).

When the law concerning the separation of Church and State came into force in 1905, the Deanery became the place of safe-keeping for the Municipal Library and the Bayeux Tapestry until 1983. As the property of the City of Bayeux, the building is now used for exhibitions periodically and various cultural activities open to the Public. The episcopal residence is now one of the mansions or town houses built in the 18th century, opposite the Cathedral, on the corner of Rue Larcher ■

Baron Gérard Museum

The former Episcopal Palace of Bayeux contains a series of Works of Arts, added to, from the end of the 18th century by the Municipality, aided by connoiseurs anxious to preserve a heritage that they are eager to share with others. The foliage of the Tree of Liberty thus gives shelter to the entrance to a museum which, since 1959 is named after one of its most generous benefactors, Baron Henri-Alexandre Gérard, nephew of the Neo-classic painter François Gérard. An Art museum; devoted to the history of the City, its considerable collections, today are centred around a number of specific art-forms : Archeological, Painting, Graphic-Arts, Furniture from the 15th to the 18th century and finally Porcelain and Bayeux Lace.

The Archeological Collections retrace the evolution of daily life in the Bayeux region for over six thousand years ; from the Neolithic period about 4500 BC to the end of the Middle Ages.
Prehistoric Bessin and the history of the Gallo-Roman City naturally take an important place, as our previous pages show. In this connection we cannot but mention the work of a great Norman archeologist, Arcisse de Caumont (1801-1873) born in Bayeux, at no. 17 Rue des Chanoines. The life and work of the Scholar, recognised by all as one of the founders of French Archeology was entirely devoted to the study and safe-keeping of the French medieval heritage. He founded the French Archeological Society in 1834 and the « Bulletin Monumental » ; as « membre correspondant » of « L'Institut », his popular works had a grest influence on his contemporaries. This was especially so in his additions to the Museum Collections, notably by the Bell known as the Fontenailles Bell, acquired by suscription in 1859. Foundered in 1202, as mentioned on the base of the bell-head, it is one of the earliest examples of the artistry of the French bell-founders. Discovered in the old

The Bell, known as the Fontenailles Bell (1202)

Parish Church of Fontenailles, it came in fact from the Benedictine Abbey of Longues-sur-Mer (near Porten-Bessin) founded in 1168 and sold as National property during the Revolution.

There are also statues from the tombs of Marie Davot and Jacques André de Sainte-Croix, works of Art by the sculptor, Jaques Lefaye (1628) placed in the Museum after the destruction of the signorial chapel in the Parish Church at Ryes (eight kilometres north of Bayeux).

The Museum also holds an exceptional collection of paintings, drawings, engravings and furniture consisting of over two thousand five hundred works. From early Italian and Flemish to contemporary artists, the greatest names in the history of Art (Floris, Momper, Champaigne, Boucher, David, Corot, Boudin, Caillebotte, Van Dongen, Utrillo, Rouault, Vlaminck...) along a line where one also comes across numerous Art-works from the great Religious Houses and private homes in Bayeux and the district around it.

One of the interesting things about the Collection without doubt is that it is largely made up of works from the Region, with much space taken up by the Northern Schools of the 16th and 17th centuries.
If we find ourselves among a myriad of lessor Masters, there are also prestigious ones as well.
Thus by the side of Italian and Spanish works, we find belonging to National Collections, two portraits from the first half of the 16th century characteristic of the Flemish School : Corneille de la Haye, known as Corneille de Lyon : «Portrait of Constable Anne de Montmorency» and «Portrait of a Chancellor of England Thomas Moore» by Hans Holbein the Elder. Beside them hang an interesting panorama of diverse works in the Landscape tradition of the 17th century Flemish School with, notably

J. de Momper (1564-1635) Famille en Voyage

«Famille en Voyage» by Joost de Momper II known as the Younger (1564-1635), «Entrée d'une forêt» by Jacques d'Arthois (1613-1655), and the two «Paysages animés au fond d'une orge» forming pendants, from the brush of David Teniers the Younger (1610-1690).

«La Vanité» by the Antwerp painter Gillis Coignet (1538-1599) takes us to other horizons. This work in which one recognises the eclectic style of a Flemish Mannerist, heavily impregnated with Italian culture, is the last vestige of the decorative cycle in the 17th century provincial home, the residence of the great de Matignon family who owned Torigni-sur-Vire (Manche), reduced to ashes in the flighting at the Liberation.

From the old Hôtel-Dieu in Bayeux came not only a very fine «Sainte-Famille» from the 17th century, but also 143 vases of its Apothecary, Faience from Rouen and Nevers and from the Midi, most of it dating from the end of the 17th and early 18th century. Among the pieces, is an exceptionally fine «chevrette» decorated in polychrome by the Rouen potter, Laurent

Chevrette in earthenware from Rouen (16th century)

Abaquesne, dating from about 1565. The Episcopal Palace in Bayeux has also given to the Museum a large collection of embroideries of the Arms of France, 17th century Parisian enbroidery , given, according to local custom by Louis XV to the Bishop, Paul d'Albert de Luynes on the occasion of his enthronement in 1729.

In the Museum collections French painting is affectd by foreign schools of Art from the second part of the 17th century. Among the major works of the period we should mention the «Charité Romaine» by Sébastien Bourdon (1616-1671) and the enigmatic «Têtes de Saint-Pierre et Saint-Paul» by Philippe de Champaigne (1602-1674) that can be compared with the design for the embroidery for the Church of Saint-Gervais and Saint-Protais in Paris done by the painter in 1657 by command of Louis XIII.

Understably, 18th century Bayeux painters are given pride of place in the Museum collections, notably Joachim Rupalley who set the tone for what can be considered as a definite Bayeux school of protrait artists that really blossomed out a generation later.

• **Joachim Rupalley** (1713-1780) came from a modest Bayeux family and learned his Art in the first third of the 18th century in the workshop of the Rouen painter Jean Restout (1692-1768) and achieved fame later as a painter in the Episcopal Court. An artist of note, his religious compositions of quality, can be seen in numerous churches in the Diocese. Among his finest works is his great portrait of Monsignor Pierre-Charles-Caesar Rochechouart, Bishop of Bayeux (1753-1776).

• **Gabriel-Narcisse Rupalley** (1746-1798) son and pupil of Joachim, was to some extent the almost official portrait-painter of the Clergy and Bajocasse Nobility. Among the canvasses of his, in the Museum, are the protraits of Marie-Antoine Fréard du Castel (1697-1771), Canon of the Cathedral, Archdeacon of Veys and famous preacher, the Chevalier Valentin Fréard du Castel, his brother, Chevalier de Saint-Louis and Lieutenant -Colonnel of the Regiment of Berry and of Monsignor de Cheylus, Bishop (1776-1791) and Mayor of Bayeux (1790) who died in exil in Jersey in 1797.

P.-F. Delaunay (1759-1789) Autoportrait au chapeau (Self-portrait wearing a hat)

• **Pierre-François Delauney** (1759-1789), son of a Bayeux hatter, left for Paris to study under Vincent and Fragonard. The young painter, permitted to exhibit in the Salons of 1787 and 1788, had the promise of a brilliant future but did not live to maturity. His «Auto-portrait au chapeau» as are also the protraits of Monsieur and Madame Anfrye demonstrate the talent of an artist who, died of tuberculous when only thirty.

• **Robert Lefèvre** (1755-1830) became renowned as a Court painter. At the age od 26 he also went to Paris and, joining the workshop of J.-B. Regnault concentrated on illustrative works, as his «Bacchante» or his «Vénus et l'Amour» shows. but he is known above all as a portrait artist of the reigning families and high dignitaries of the Empire and after that, the Restoration. The portrait of the politician Jacques-Antoine Manuel (1775-1827) is one of the works most representative of him.

R. Lefèvre (1755-1830) Bacchante

The canvasses of the Museum collections make it possible to follow the History of Art in parallel from the best sources, showing the rapid evolution of French Painting from the end of the «Ancien Régime». This goes through three stages, after the suave elegance of Art at Court at the end of the reign of Louis XV comes the decisive rupture, heralding the emergence of Neoclassicism in the years preceeding the Revolution, followed during the first decades of the 19th century by the first ripples of Romanticism. The contrast is quite startling if one puts in perspective «La Cage» by François Boucher (1768), with a study of «Philosophe» by Jacques-Louis David (1779), «Sapho à Leucate» by Antoine-Jean Gros (1801) or again, «Hylas et la Nymphe» by François Gérard (1825-1826).

The Museum offers a real panorama of diverse currents of 19th century French Painting, chosen by two great Norman lovers of Art who had at times differing tastes but which was profondly complementary. They were : first of all Baron Henri-Alexandre Gérard (1818-1903), archetype of the grand bourgeois of the second part of the 19th century to whom we owe the Neoclassic Collection of the Museum.

F. Boucher La Cage (detail) (1768)

The collection he put in place constitutes a very good guide to French 19th century Painting. Along side the canvasses of David, Gros end Gérard, one finds the works of Michel-Martin Drolling, Georges Michel, Jean-Emile-Horace Vernet, Jacques-Raymond Brascassat, Eugène Fromentin, Georges Moreau de Tours, Rodolphe Ribarz, or again Victor Gilbert.

The Collection we owe to Doctor Eugène Jacquette (1829-1899) is quite different, more informal in some sense intimate. From 1870 onwards Jacquette and his wife had friendships with their contemporaries in the Art-world some of whom gave them dedicated works, notably Eugène Boudin (1824-1898), Camille Corot (1796-1875) or Théodule Ribot (1823-1891). Some of these dedicated works are still in Bayeux today.

Boudin's friendship is apparent on his work «La Rue à Fervaques» dated 30th July 1881 and dedicated to «A l'ami Jacquette» : it was painted during a time when he stayed at a place that belonged to Jacquette near Livarot.

The Museum has also the good fortune to have «Portraits à la campagne» a major work of the painter Gustave Caillebotte (1848-1894) exhibited in April 1877 at the third exhibiiton of the Impressionists. Donated to the Museum by M. and Mme Chaplin of Bayeux, relatives of the Artist, it is one of the very few canvasses of this painter in French public collections. The influence of the Impresssionists is very perceptible in the series of paintings in the Museum. It is particularly so in the Norman Painter Jules-Louis Rame (1855-1927) and is largely in evidence. In the research done on optical analysis in colour and light, it is equally represented by the artists of the Pointillist Movement from the middle of the eighteen-eighties of which «Fleurs dans un vase» by Henri-Edmond Delacroix or Cross (1856-1910) is a perfect example.

The Graphic Art of the 19th and 20th centuries has also a privileged place in the Museum. One finds some quite elegant examples of life under the Second Empire in Lower Normandy and others less so, in the large number of exhibits from artists coming from this region, such as François Maugendre (1809-1895), Thomas-Casimir Regnault (1823-187), or Septime Le Pippre (1833-1871). As to Art in the 20th century, the library of prints and engravings constitues an essential part of the path along which French Art in painting, has travelled. Among the finer plates, numerous examples abound, born of the collaboration of the Art Editor, Edmond Frapier with Pierre Bonnard, Maurice Denis, Felix Othon-Friez, Aristide Maillol, Georges Rouault, Kees Van Dongen or Maurice de Vlaminck.

Where contemporary Art is concerned the collection of engravings is extraordinarily wide and rich in variety.

L. Mouillet
The enamelling workshop in the manufacture of porcelain

Finally, the Museum very ably demonstrates the skill and commitment of the makers of porcelain and lace who have made Bayeux famous everywhere in the sphere of Applied Arts.

Throughout its history, the City of Bayeux has encouraged the development of decorative Arts. One of their great successes in this, was the beginning in 1812, of porcelain manufacture. From the first porcelain of Lower Normandy, made at Valognes (Manche) between 1802 and 1812 by the head of a Bayeux Porcelain Firm, Joachim Langlois, came the fine blue red and gold Bayeux china of the early 19th century. After that came the Polychrome porcelain of François Gosse, in the Eclectic style of the time of Napoleon III. From 1878 the Morlent family produced Blue Cobalt Monochrome porcelain with delicate designs until mid 20th century when the kilns finally ceased to be fired. The century and a half of Bayeux porcelain has been faithfully recorded by the Museum. This long page in Bayeux history we shall return to, later on.

L. Panchet La Dentellière

In the last century Bayeux was also one of the great Lace-making centres of Europe. Introduced into Bayeux at the end of the 17th century, Lace-making reached its zenith during the 19th century. The Museum unravels for the visitors the abundance and extraordinary quality of this lace, entirely hand-made : scarfs, flounces, kerchiefs, shawls, lace-edging or accessory rimmings in blonde lace, unbleached, or black Chantilly destined for the European Upper Class and exported world wide. The Museum collections make it possible to study in detail aspects of technique and commerce in on of the more famous lace-making houses of the Second Empire, that of the Lefébure family.

The extent of the work-force consisting of thousands of lace-makers, working at home in dreadful and precarious conditions, well merits the space devoted to it, in the pages that follow ■

Ombrelle en Chantilly
(Parasol in Chantilly Lace)
made in Bayeux about 1860

G. Caillebotte (1848-1894) Portraits à la campagne (Country Portraits) (1876)

V. Gilbert (1847-1933) La Demoiselle

H. Cross (1856-1910) Fleurs dans un vase
(Flowers in a vase)

When, under Philippe Auguste, Normandy reverted to the French Crown in 1204, there began, a century marked by prosperity in the countryside and the development of urban economy. This period was without doubt when ecclesiastical power reached its zenith in the City economy. The City's prosperity and the influence of the Bishops were often closely related to the Royal Power, notably under Saint Louis, Philippe le Hardi and Philippe le Bel : particularly noticeable was the vast building-works that took place in the Cathedral.

The Priory Gateway of Saint-Vigor-le-Grand

About twenty parish churches or chapels existed in the City. Of the six that were within the walls, only the vestiges of Saint-Nicolas-des-Courtils remains, situated at the end of an alley, opening on to Rue Général-de-Dais. Outside the walls on Mount Phaunus the Benedictine Priory of Saint-Vigor-le-Grand has been restored and one can still admire the fine gateway and the barn that dates from the end of the 13th century.

There were of course the new Religious Houses like the Hôtel-Dieu founded by Bishop Robert des Ablèges (1206-1231) outside the City gates, put in the hands of the Canons Regular of Saint Augustin. The chapel of their former convent, the interior of which is a very fine example of 13th century Gothic, has been preserved ; it is entered through the courtyard of the Tapestry Museum.

From the second third of the 14th century the situation was such more sombre, marked by the enfeeblement, both financial and political of royal power. Normandy was caught up in he main thrust of the first onslaught of the Hundred years War which started in

The former convent chapel of the Augustinian Canons

July 1346, when Avranches, Saint-Lô and Caen were taken by Edward III, King of England, as pretender to the Throne of France. Although Bayeux remained untouched, the outskirts and surrounding country in the Bessin suffered destruction and pillage. Added to this were periods of scarcity and the Black Death that made its apperance for the first time in 1348. In spite of these catastrophies and all kinds of difficulties the old City, protected by its walls and castle with its garrison, escaped destruction.

Wood and plaster, serve too often perhaps, to characterise the Bayeux of the Middle Ages. There are however, numerous edifices, notably in the Canonical Quarter that have come down to us from the 15th century, showing that in medieval times not only ecclesiastical and military construction was in stone but also a considerable number of private houses.

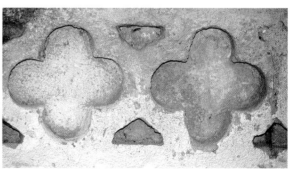

Quadrilobes decorate the facade of the Church of Saint-Nicolas

Above the roofs of the houses bordering the Parvis of the Cathedral emerges a rather strange cyclinder of stone crowned by a series of «colonnettes» supporting a conical roofing perforated with round holes. Long known as «Lanterne des Morts», it is in fact a chimney, a surprising remnant of a 13th century dwelling which

Canon's residence at no.13 Rue de la Maîtrise

today is completely integrated into the structeure of the 18th century houses that have replaced it.

One of the finest examples of this medieval architectural tradition can be seen in the houe at nos. 11-13 Rue de la Maîtrise, probably the residence of a 14th century canon. It is very much in character, built of small blocks of marneu limestone carefully laid, with stones almost touching. The facade on the upper floor still has windows with stone cross-pieces and lintels with trilobic arcading. Notable to is the cornice with fur-leaf decoration that runs along the base of the roof, above which rises the stair-turret.

Looking closely at the facade of no. 15 in the same street one notices four lancet windows, two of which have been restored and two sealed up, on both sides are counterforts in light relief. These windows and their decorative stone-work show them to have once been part of a private chapel in a house which, though very much altered, certainly dates from the Gothic period.

The oldest wood-and-plaster house in Bayeux, that has come down to us, stands at the corner of Rue des Cuisiniers and Rue Saint-Martin. Dating from the 14th century, it has quadrilobic decoration on its sculptured chimney-stack.

The wood-and-plaster structure (Colombage) has a front gable with windows supported by cross-pieces. Stout over-hanging woodwork supports the two upper-floors. These are supported by short pillars on the ground-floor with supporting stone-base. The stair-case alongside is set back slightly, consisting of dressed-stone and limestone-rubble. The intervening woodwork and the limestone filling between each beam-apparent is light and fragile.

In medieval times the ground-floor of the house, used as a shop, had its openings protected from the falling rain by the succession of overlapping floors making life more pleasant.

If other buildings of the same type appear to date from

the 14th century, higher up the Grand-rue, on the corner of Rue Saint-Martin and the Rue Franche or Rue des Cuisiniers at no.20 or in the courtyard of no.8, these wood-and-plaster houses are not medieval ; the City officials did not forbid their construction until 1650 onwards.

Wood-and-plaster house at no. 1 Rue des Cuisiniers

A. Maugendre
1876

A. Maugendre del.

Bayeux.

Cour de la maison N.º 4, rue S.ᵗ Malo.

Staircase Tower at the town house «L'hôtel de Rubercy» no. 5 Rue Franche

When in 1415 the English King Henry V forced the gates of the towns of Lower Normandy there began in Bayeux a period of thirty-three years in which the population were under English rule. One of the major figures of the time was undoutedly, Alain Chartier (1385-1433) who used his talents both as poet and diplomat with the Dauphin Charles (the future Charles VII). The author of «Quadriloge invectif» and of «Traité de l'espérance», unlike his brother Guillaume, Archbishop of Paris, he did not assist in the liberation of Normandy. The enterprise in which King Charles VII engaged happened between 1449 and 1450. The outcome was the Battle of Formigny on 14th April 1450 followed by the siege of Bayeux where the Captain of the English garrison was shut in with his troops. Led by the Count of Dunois, the garrison surrended in about twelve days. On the 16th May, King Charles VII granted a full and complete amnesty to all the City's inhabitants.

The end of the Hundred Years War was, in every sense for the old City, the Renaissance. This was true economically but also for the new masters. The ancient lineages, whether aristocracy or bourgeoisie had largely died out, decimated by wars and plague, exiled or simply ruined. In a few generations, fortune had passed into new hands, who, as peace had definitely returned, wished to make their mark on the City and surrounding country.

This gratifying state of affairs developed from the middle of the fifteen century and probably reached its peak between the years 1475 and 1525. The period of architectural renaissance came from the medieval tradition, where the Flamboyant Gothic largely dominated.

The most characteristic element was, without doubt, the Manor house. It consisted of a rectangular building of two floors with a built-on turret containing a spiral staircase, that served, with a single flight of stairs, each floor up to the roof. The staircase from this time on, was pushed outside the house into a tower that jutted out from the main building. At its base, usually hexagonal, it was square as it moved upwards, terminating in a little room that overhangs the rest and has a span roof.

In the 15th century the window-frames with crosspieces were frequently adorned with mouldings and

Decorated beams of the mansion : Grand hôtel d'Argouges at no. 4 Rue Saint-Malo

The «bas-relief» on a tower,
Impasse Saint-Nicolas,
Rue Général-de-Dais

elaborate head-pieces as were the doors with ornamental arcading on the lintels, some with curled-leaf decoration. The cornice beneath the gutter was sometimes decorated with a beautiful twisted fringe or cord. Gable ends and towers often had decoration in scroll or cabbage-leaf form, or Lion and Chimera in high relief.

There are still some sixty of these mansions and manor houses around the centre of the City, dating from this period (streets : Rue Franche no.5 and 18, Rue de la Juridiction no. 3-5 and 32, Saint-Malo no. 4-8 and 60, Saint Martin no. 44-46, des Cuisiniers no. 18 and 25, du Bienvenu no. 2, Bourbesneur no. 10) and in the «faubourgs» (i.e. outside the walls, Rue Saint Jean, courtyard of no. 53, Rue de la Cambette no.1, and Rue Montfiquet no. 13 and 23).

Whilst some are built with dressed stone, most are of limestone rubble and some have a wood and plaster facade facing the street, the wood richly carved. Only two remain just as they were, for us to see the whole cycle of the decoration. That of the «grand hôtel» d'Argouges (no. 7 rue Saint-Malo) is completely composed of figures of saints. One the ground-floor, framed in the wall on the left is a statue of the Virgin under a canopy and on the right a figure of Saint John the Baptist. On the first floor (from left to right), easily visible is : Christ with Saint Mary Magdaleine on her knees, Saint Barbara and her tower, Saint Catherine crowned with her wheel, Saint Martha with the monster at her feet, with finally a last figure difficult to make out. On the second level, only three of the six are identifiable : the third, fourth end sixth, beginnig on the left : Saint Côme carrying his pot of oinment, Saint Laurence and his grid-iron and finally Saint Roche and his dog and not, as far as one can make out : Saint Anthony and his pig.

The second floor of «La Maison d'Adam et Eve» is equally «consacré au monde sacré». From left to right is : Archangel Gabriel with a sword, Adam, the Tree of sin and the serpent, Eve and finally the stoning of Saint Stephen. On the second floor the illusrations are secular consisting of allegorical or mythological subjects, from left to right : a siren holding a mirror, a unicorn,

a shepherd, Venus from a ripple carried by a wave, finally a lion or some monstrous animal. The sculptures on the ground-floor are a modern addition.

Sculpture in the form of stained-glass windows no. 19 of Rue des Cuisiniers

Few of the Bayeux mansions have the characteristics of the Renaissance as such. The most remarkable elements of that influence date from the first half of the 16th century; to be found in the stone-work around doors and windows : rectangular columns with geometrical motifs, crowned with elegant capitals, finely loulded and very fine sculpture (notably no. 9, Rue Général-de-Dais).

Sculpture above a window no. 60 of Rue Saint-Malo

The one edifice that is real Renaissance is the Church-tower of Saint-Patrice, seven stories high, built between 1544 and 1548. There is square stone-work, plain at the base, each stage narrowing, having individual form, rich ornamented cornices and pillars, with successive styles of Doric, Ionic and Corinthian. The tower from square to circular and finally to three superimposed cupolas ∎

Renaissance Décor no.9 Rue Général-de-Dais

Saint-Patrick's bell-tower

Normandy in the second half of the 16th century was dominated by a confrontation between those representing Roman Catholic doctrine and those of the Calvinist reform movement who had gained the support of large numbers of the «petite noblesse» and «bourgeoisie» in Lower Normandy.

The conflict reached a state of paroxysm in 1562-1563. Faced with rioting, the clergy and Royal Authority representatives fled, leaving the insurgents masters of the City for several months. The gold and silver plate of the Cathedral and Episcopal Palace was melted down, whilst throughout the City, all things sacred (altars, statues, choir-stalls, stained-glass windows...) were smashed.

The state of civil war abated rapidly but long years were needed to heal the wounds, kept alive at the same time by chronic poverty under the incessant rise of taxation.

Portrait of
Monsignor de Nesmond
(Baron Gérard Museum)

Not until the first decades of the 17th century was the centralised power of Royal Authority restored, acompanied by the reforms of the Council of Trent put in place by the Episcopate.

The founding of new eligious Orders follo-wed (five in Bayeux between 1615 and 1650). A new religious climate was desti-ned to reinvigorate the spiritual education of the people. The arrival of these Orders in Bayeux was clearly marked in the context of the Counter-reformation.

Each Order played a part in the life of the respective «faubourg» outside the City-walls. These Religious communities were housed in large conventual buildings which, despite many alterations since, have survived for the most part, to this day. From the middle of the 17th century there are : the former Benedictine convent (fronting Rue Maurice-Schumann), Sisters of Our Lady of Charity (facing Place Gauquelin-des-Pallieres), and the Ursulines convent, (the facade of no. 9 Rue Saint-Patrice).

Each Religious Order had its own peculiarity but all were known for their strict rule of life. There was, in the same context, an ambitious architectural programme undertaken in the reign of Louis XIV by Monsignor François de Nesmond (1662-1715). This saw the founding of the General Hospital, the impo-sing gateway of which dates from 1676 ; the date is ins-cribed on the main entrance in Rue Saint-Jean (oppo-site no. 125). The Hospital was followed by the buil-ding of the Seminary (now the Tapestry Museum).

Stone in the courtyard of the
General Hospital Rue Saint-Jean

Arms of Monsignor Nesmond
Allée des Augustines

Facade of the former Convent of the Sisters of Charity
facing courtyard Place Gauquelin-Despallières

The Seminary, Allée des Augustines viewed from the entrance

The establishment was entrusted to the Lazarist Brothers, and the first stone was laid in 1693. Finally, started in 1696 was the renovation of the conventual buildings of the Sisters recently put in charge of running the Hôtel-Dieu (Allée des Augustines). There was a noticeable austerity of style in the renovation that looked at closely, follows the lines of French architecture in the lay sphere ; all trace of the ornamental, was removed from the facades.

The City was a wealth of different trends in French architecture, from the end of the reign of Louis XIII (1610-1643), up to the first hiccups of the Revolution.

Agricultural progress from the beginning of the 17th century is very noticeable in Normandy. In the countryside around Bayeux cattle-breeding on permanent pasture-land allowed for the progressive development of salted butter. At the gates of Bayeux, on the road to Tilly-sur-Seulles, Crémel, a splendid farm house, is a fine example of the imposing manor-houses of the first decades of the 17th century, that illustrate the wealth of the rural landowners of the Bessin, in contrast to the splendid residences that the great seigneurs like Jean de Choisy at Balleroy or Jacques Turgot at Lantheuil built for temselves.

In imitation of their country cousins, wealthy bourgeois and Nobles of the long Robe, enriched by the growth in the number of Royal functions built themselves new residences. The increase in number of these private mansions left the lay-out of medieval Bayeux unchanged, but it set the tone in new ideas of classic French architecture. Leaving aside certain archaic details, such as some inordinately high roofs, the oldest of these mansions have a style related to that of the end of the reign of Louis XIII and the beginnig of the reign of Louis XIV (namely, between 1630 and 1670) ; the most interesting examples are those found in the streets : Rue de la Maitrise (no. 17), des Ursulines (no. 9), Général-de-Dais (no. 18-20), Franche (no. 9), Saint Malo (no. 2 and 27), Saint-Jean (no. 53) and Saint-Patrice (no. 56).

Dormer window at no. 9 Rue des Ursulines

Sculpture over the gateway of no. 87 Rue Saint-Jean

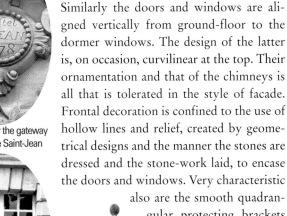

Window at no. 17 Rue de la Maîtrise

The arrangement of space in the house interiors consisted of rooms leading into one another though each with a particular function (bedroom, study, library, dining-room...) and this is clearly perceptible from outside through the large windows of the facades on all the floors.

The severity of the architectural design of the buildings is striking. The different floors are marked by a band of stone, usually in relief, running the length of the building. Similarly the doors and windows are aligned vertically from ground-floor to the dormer windows. The design of the latter is, on occasion, curvilinear at the top. Their ornamentation and that of the chimneys is all that is tolerated in the style of facade. Frontal decoration is confined to the use of hollow lines and relief, created by geometrical designs and the manner the stones are dressed and the stone-work laid, to encase the doors and windows. Very characteristic also are the smooth quadrangular protecting brackets placed under the cornices of the roofs and at the top of imposing chimney-stacks.

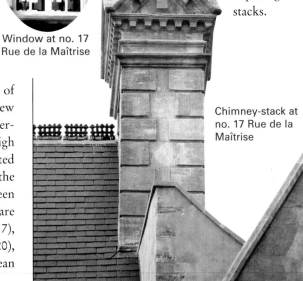

Chimney-stack at no. 17 Rue de la Maîtrise

It will be noticed that throughout the City are numerous gateways in a particular style of architecture where the decoration is completed by motifs ending with a diamond point and seldom with a scroll. Only in the last third of the 18th century that the influence of the great French architects in the service of Louis XIV at Versailles is noticeable. In the Bessin it can be seen in the work of the Bayeux architect Jacques Moussard (1670-1750), a Royal architect, influenced by the work of Jules-Hardouin Mansart. Among his works in Bayeux are : Place Saint-Patrice, the facade of the Convent Chapel of the Sisters of Our Lady of Charity (circa 1706-1708) and the fine «Hôtel de Castilly» (no. 10 Rue Général-de-Dais).

For this residence in prescribed, almost perfect, classic style, the architect knew how to work within the constraints imposed by the general lay-out of the City. Built, backing on to the City ramparts, it had a terrace on the first floor that overlooked the rampart moat, later grassed over. The main facade faced the street, fronted by an elegant «Cour d'honneur» (main courtyard). The whole, consists of the main building set back slightly from the two sides surmounted by a much embellished piece of sculpture that once displayed the Arms of the family residing there (the Faudoas family). Nowhere else in Bayeux architecture are there such high windows. In constrast with other windows and doors, surmounted with segmented arcs, this, in the absence of a central balcony, has three semi-circular bay windows ornamented with ladies' masques and helmets, heightening the prestigious air of the central section of the facade.

Few residences possess characteristics comparable to those in this fine edifice but there is another, though of a more intimate character : La Crespellière (no. 7 Rue Franche), the residence of Bon-François-Bonaventure Crespel, King's Advocate for the Bailiwick, Alderman then Mayor of Bayeux between 1759 and 1760.
Otherwise, many buildings of the second third of the 18th century show refined taste (a main aspect of the Louis XV style) that progressively took over from the grandiose character inherited from the century of Louis XIV.

From them on, there was a profusion of ornamental motifs on the facades often very elaborate, with a basis in shells and lockets in a frame-work of scrolls in a complex and repetitive design. In the imposing character of «l'hôtel de Royville» (no. 14 Rue Royale), is a contrast to the intimate character of the house known as, Maison de la du Barry (no. 39-41 Rue Larcher) or again «de la Bonbonnière» (no. 1 Rue des Ursulines). The entasis in design of the central building gives great charm in each of them. In «l'hôtel Tillard-des-Acres» (no. 36 Rue des Bouchers) this effect is obtained by the wrought-iron grills on the windows.

If a great number of buildings in Bayeux have windows with a head-piece of segmented arcs, giving them the appearance of dating from the second third of the 18th century, most are earlier buildings that were altered later. Less prestigious than the former, some are nevertheless of real quality (no. 23 Rue Général-de-Dais, no. 56 Rue Saint-Malo, no. 34 Rue Saint-Martin, no. 19 Rue de la Maîtrise or no.16 Rue de Nesmond). The last third of the 18th century saw the end of the use by Bayeux architects of the once very elegant ornamental descriptions but they were rigorous in their use of the Louis XVI style. This is very standardised and found in number of buildings throught the City. Like other buildings, Mansions (known as «hôtels particuliers») are built right on to the street. The facade, usually with an imposing balcony of wrought iron is frequently ornamented on two or three floors by pillars ; plain or fluted and, almost always with rectangular panels within which are garlands of drapery or foliage with or without ribbon frilling.

Among the finest mansions in this style is the mighty «hôtel de la Tour du Pin» former residence of the Bricqueville family (no. 14 Rue Général-de-Dais) with its main courtyard at the rear of the building, «l'hôtel du Cadran» (no. 6 Rue Saint-Martin), the residence of a wealthy ironmonger, it was built about 1795. There are some modest dwellings (no. 64 and 76 Rue des Bouchers, no. 12 Rue des Chanoines), with simple doorways (no. 58 Rue des Cuisiniers, no. 6 Rue Royale), notice too some rather modest buildings (no. 18 Rue Saint-Martin, no. 9 Rue des Cuisiniers).

Hôtel de Castilly, no.10 Rue Général-de-Dais

La Crespellière no. 7
Rue Franche

Former Ursuline Convent no. 69
Rue Saint-Patrice

La Bonbonnière no. 69
Rue des Ursulines

House known as Maison
de la du Barry
no. 39-41 Rue Larcher

Hôtel Tillard-
des-Acres
no. 36 Rue
des Bouchers

Balcony on the
Corner of Rue
Larcher and Rue
Saint-Jean

Hôtel du Cadran
at no. 6
Rue Saint-Martin

Hôtel de la Tour-du-Pin
no. 14 Rue Général-de-Dais

47

Gateway of the old General
Hospital Rue Saint-Jean

Doorway of no. 87 Rue Saint-Jean

The Episcopal Palace Rue Laitière

Doorway of no. 132 Rue Saint-Jean

Doorway of no. 17 Rue des Ursulines

Doorway of no. 6 Rue Bourbesneur

Doorway of no. 2 Rue des Ursulines

Doorway of no. 2 Rue de la Maîtrise

Doorway of no. 11 Rue Franche

The taking down of the old ramparts continued apace, the gates were torn down, the moats were progressively filled in, became building-plots or were laid out as gardens. Despite ambitious projects, the medieval castle, raised to the ground as a concession to the Municipality by Louis XVI in 1773, were unfulfilled and the urban development envisaged, did not take place. The only public projects that did, were : the building of the bridge of Saint-Jean in the extended Grand-rue and the rebuilding of the «Halle aux viandes», Rue Saint-Martin, with the re-arrangement of the area in the immediate vicinity.

Bayeux was, at the end of the 18th century a City of little more than 10 000 inhabitants. Two-thirds of the heads of families were tradesmen or artisans to which should be added not less than 600 domestics. The middle-classes were numerous, since, out of 1 300 dwellings there were 1 257 property-owners.

Sculptured stone-work on the gateway of the Halle aux Viandes, Rue Saint-Martin

Only 10% of the population came from Noble Families and Royal Officers, most of whom resided close to the Castle. So that in Rue Général-de-Dais we find : Augustin Hervé de Faudoas, Marquis de Canisy, Lieutenant of the Gendarmerie and his wife Isabelle de Bernières ; Count Pierre d'Albiniac, Lieutenant Colonel of the Queens Regiment of Dragoons and his wife Madeleine de Bailleul; Marquis Henri de Bricqueville, also an officer in the Dragoons and his wife Charlotte d'Harcourt ; Augustin Alexandre de Saffray, Knight of Saint-Louis, Governor of the Port of Isigny, husband of Marguerite de Bailleul, also Gilles Edouard de Marguerye, Seigneur of Vierville, Houtteville and Formigny, husband of Anne de Pleurre.

During his Episcopate (1776-1791), Bishop Joseph-Dominique de Cheylus was First Chaplain to Madame Duchesse d'Artois and Mayor of Bayeux in 1790 when the Revolution took hold. Refusing to accept the new arrangements imposed by the revolutionary government, notably the civil arrangement regarding clergy, he was forced to go into exile in Jersey in 1791 where he died in 1797. He was succeeded in Bayeux by Claude Fauchet who accepted the new system and was deputed by the Legislative Assembly as representative of Calvados. He was later accused of complicity in the Charlotte Corday affair and executed on 31st October 1793. There occured at this point profound social changes. Religious Communities were dissolved, Clerical possessions, like those of the «Emigrés» (those who had fled abroad) were seized and sold as public goods, or transferred to the secular power.

As to the Cathedral, it became The Temple of Reason, later of The Supreme Being. A number of voices were raised on behalf of the rich historic heritage of the ancient City. First of all it was Lambert Leforestier who saved the Tapestry from vandalism, then members of the Arts Commission, acting at District level, who saved thousands of books and hundreds of works of Art, History and Science from the buildings, taken over. After 1794, the Commission envisaged the creation of a museum in which, works of value could be collected, notably those made up of the Cathedral Treasures. The historic and artistic importance of that precious archive illustrating the conquest of England was coveted by many. Amongst the various claimants, Bonaparte himself, made the decision. The First Consul took note of the care taken by the People of Bayeux, for its conservation over the seven and a half centuries and placed it firmly in their custody in February 1804.

The Native Land of Bon-Claude Cahier de Gerville (1751-1796) Minister of the Interior under Louis XVI, to whom the establishment of Civil Registers is attributed, the Painter Robert Lefèvre (1756-1830) and Arcisse de Caumont (1802-1873), founder of French Archeology, comes out badly from an economic standpoint, enfeebled by the tumult of the Revolution. It was nevertheless a time when the Country acquired a new dimension, a vital step forward for the lover of History and Art, whether erudite or merely curious ■

Among the many writers who came to Bayeux during the 19th Century, such as Honoré de Balzac (1779-1850) who stayed with his sister Madame Surville in the summer of 1822, it is to Théophile Gautier (1811-1872) who came to the City in August 1858 that we owe one of the most interesting accounts of the atmosphere of it, published in «Quand on Voyage» in 1865. Mainly concerning the textile indutry and lace-making particularly, the population remained stable from the end of the 18th century until the early 1850's. From then on, with the collapse of manufacturing and consequently the emigration of the male workforce, the population declined throughout the second half of the century. Life in Bayeux can be seen from the text of Théophile Gautier *«In our time of industrial breathlessness, it is a rare thing to see in a city, peacefully grouped around its cathedral without factory chimneys intermingled with its bell towers, people stretching their arms out, in sheer provincial boredom, not without charm and at least, leaving long hours for reverie.»*

To municipal authority, after the Revolution, had been left the running and transformation of the City. In the hands therefore of the «Bourgeoisie», members of the Council came mainly from property-owners, the liberal professions and traders. The latter, whether in the public or private domain, make their mark on the character of a modern city. Here as chief town, in the surrounding countryside depended on the exploitation of rich agricultural land, one of the best in Normandy.

With the coming of the Railway in 1858, gas-lighting in 1886, then in 1913 electric-light, the City acquired a number of monuments that from then on formed an integral part of the City landscape. European conflicts in this period affected profoundly, the City-fathers and People alike. Two monuments recall the sorrow felt by the wars of 1870-1871 (the work of Arthur Le Duc situated at the corner of Rue de la Poterie and Rue Maurice-Schumann) and 1914-1918 (the work of the sculptor Eugène Bénet, Avenue de la Vallée-des-Prés), both dedicated to the conflicts subsequently.

The episcopal status of Bayeux was renewed in 1901 with the joint dioceses of Bayeux and Lisieux. The clergy abounded since in the City were two hundred priests, monks and nuns, added to which were about a hundred pupils in the «Grand Séminaire». Théophile Gautier underlines the influence exercised by the presence of *«priests who go here and there just like in Rome»*, on the atmosphere of a city that «has something ecclesiastical in its tranquility and repose».

From the end of the 18th century, the straightening of some of the streets and development of some points allowed for a harmonious advance for its medieval heart. The tradesmen had the help of the City architects who assisted in the restoration of the facades of shops and houses.

The commercial «Grand-Rue» and adjacent streets became privileged as a walk-about, providing a display of domestic architecture from the Restoration to the very end of the Second Empire. With the advantage of porcelain manufacture within its walls the Municipality adopted, in the first decades of the 19th century a system of marking and numbering, streets and houses displayed on plaques of white porcelain, inscribed by hand on each. These can still be seen.

One characteristic trait in the 19th century architecture and the first part of the 20th is the progressive use of classic sources leading to an eclectic style in which by the second part of the century ornamental vagetation held a dominant place. In the religious domain, heavily inspired by the medieval period, Gothic triumphed. The noblest of materials were used : dressed stone-work and forged-iron, joined in the second part of the 19th century by other components, notably ceramics, cast-iron and hand-worked zinc, whilst at the dawn of the 20th century, wood, claimed an honoured place. The introduction of reinforced-concrete was one of the main acquisitions of the first part of the 20th century.

Amongst the great innovations at the end of the Restoration was the advent of restaurants and the opening of the old theatre (now a cinema, Rue Genas-Duhomme) where, amongst other productions in 1840, was the celebrated Bayeux tragedienne Georges Wiemmer (1787-1867) who came to fame in

The old Halle aux Poissons (Fish market) Bridge of Saint-Jean

Paris when barely fourteen, on the stage of the present Comédie Française. The facade of the Bayeux theatre was designed by the architect Edouard Leforestier (1790-1851) and built in 1830, in the classical style. Under the broad front of the main section of the building with its sculptured symbols of theatre are the great arcades which were current features of urban architecture of the period. The City architect, Edouard Lair de Bauvais (1790-1851) used it for the gateway of the Halle aux Grains (corn market) 1830 and the entrance to the Halle aux Poissons (fish market) (1845-1850) ; both were built in Rue Saint-Jean.

These are perfect examples of utilitarian architecture of the second third of the 19th century, marked by their extreme austerity of design, very noticeable in the extreme severity of l'Hôtel de Police (Police station) (Place de la Liberté) built by the architect for Calvados about 1840. In the first part of the century, Classic architecutre was also the rule for domestic building and to some extent later on. Among its main characteristics there was a pronounced taste for wide cornices with mouldings or arch supports.

There were also, balconies, triangular tops to facades, doors and sometimes windows, heavy scroll-work was often used to support the head-piece. A gallery above the ground-floor formed a base for the windows of the first floor.

The decoration was usually shells with scrolls and foliage or Grecian ; pillars with geometric designs were also common. (no. 5 Rue Saint-Malo, no. 9 Rue Saint Martin, no. 12, 46 and 80 Rue Saint-Jean and no. 17 Rue Laitière).

The Sous-Prefecture (Bayeux has a Sub Prefet) is a mansion in itself, built between 1862 and 1864 on a design by the architect Leon Marcotte (1822-1885) and conceived as such. It is a magnificent example from the Napoleon III period, of an official residence. The change in taste is very fickle between the years 1840-1850. It appears to have a depletion of contrast between different sections and from then on we find very elegant ornamentation, characteristically based on a floral arrangement of bouquets, foliage and petals, either inset or in relief, under the

Façade of no.56-62 Rue des Cuisiniers

cornices and on raised surfaces of walls, also with panels of geometric designs (house at the corner of Rue Général-de-Dais and Place Charles-de-Gaulle, no. 78 and no. 71 Rue Saint-Malo the latter is dated 1857, no. 52 Rue Saint-Martin unfortunately, damaged but dated 1858 and marked : Alphonse Delaunay (1818-1886), no. 84 Rue des Bouchers, no. 6 Rue Alain-Chartier and also no. 56-62 Rue des Cuisiniers).

Facade of no. 20 Rue Saint-Martin

Sous-Préfecture, Place Charles de Gaulle

The evolution continued in the years 1870-1900 influenced by the balneal, with an unbridled taste for ornamentation; the fine property at no. 105 rue Saint-Jean, in the style of Charles Le Verrier (1822-1885) is a good example. Elsewhere sculpture in bas or haut-relief around windows or the topping of dormer windows with a diversity of materials (ceramic, cast-iron and carved woodwork) are the main characteristics (no. 52 and the Lion d'Or Hôtel, Rue Saint-Jean, l'hôtel du Luxembourg, Rue des Bouchers, the decoration of no. 75 and 59, in Rue Saint-Malo, also the house at no. 1 Rue Tardif dated 1900). The old «Hôtel des Postes» (post office) (at no. 12 and 12bis Rue Laitière) built in 1883 is one of the most interesting «administrative» buildings of the 3rd Republic, and represents a good example of this eminently eclectic style.

Facade of no. 75 Rue Saint-Malo

Art Nouveau Decor at no. 10 Rue Tardif

Residence at no. 105 Rue Saint-Jean

Shop-front at no. 2 Rue Laitière

Likewise, the parallel course of Religious Architecture in the second part of the 19th century saw in Bayeux the development of the Neogothic ; a fervent devotee of this was Alexandre Noget-Lacoudre (1806-1868), both architect and priest. To him we owe the Chapel of the Community of the Misericorde (now a presbytery, no. 4 Rue Général-de-Dais) and that of the Benedictine Nuns (no. 48 Rue Saint-Loup) built respectively in 1863 and 1865. Before moving on, from Religious Architecture the extensive cycle of Saint-Sulpice decor dedicated to the Saint-Bishops of Bayeux, is worthy of a mention, noting : Saint-Patrice, the chapels of the Augustine Nuns, the Great Seminary and also «La Charité» at Saint-Vigor-le-Grand, all of which were restored at the same period as the Cathedral in the second part of the 19th century.

The Convent of the Benedictine Nuns at no. 48 Rue Saint-Loup

Architecture known as Art Nouveau is scarcely noticeable in Bayeux (an exception is the old «garage automobile in Rue Tardif»). The taste for «wood-and-plaster» style was a characteristic trait, over the years 1890-1920. In Bayeux it is to be found largely on the periphery (notably in the vicinity of the «Maison d'accueil» of Parc Michel d'Ornano, though also at no. 8 Rue des Bouchers and 38bis Rue Nesmond). These, in conception illustrate a style that is neo-regionalistic, with a charm born of assembling wings and gables and the diversity of the materials used : real or arificial tinted timbers with matching brickwork or silex, tiled roofs, ornate ridge-tile-ends and various other embellishments in ceramic polychrome.

The development of re-inforced concrete in the first half of the 20th century made new devices possible. One of the oldest buildings of this genre, still intact is on the corner of Rue Saint-Martin and Rue Laitière. Steeped heavily in the architectural style of the great Paris stores, the edifice consists of three floors opening on to wide bays each with a surrounding decor of vegetation-moulding and crowned with an ovoid cupola, clad with slate and ornamental zinc. Another, though later shopfront of note, typical of the Thirties is «Le Vêtement Moderne» (no. 65 Rue Saint-Malo) which contrasts strongly with the elegance and even balance of the edifice so typically Art Deco at no. 1 Boulevard Sadi-Carnot. Finally, concluding this section we draw your attention to an astonishing piece of architecture of distinction, built in 1942 by the architect H. Leboullanger no.. 31bis Rue Larcher) which is the oldest example of this type of architecture to be found in Bayeux ∎

Former Store «Le Vêtement Moderne» at no. 65 Rue Saint-Malo

Maison d'accueil at Parc Michel d'Ornano

Bayeux Porcelain

Porcelain is a specific type of ceramic. It can only be made with white fireproof clay, known as Kaolin, composed of silica alumina and powdered granite. To this is added a solvent (feldspath, carbonate of lime) ; heated to a temperature of 1 410° it vitrifies. A ceramic is produced that is white, non-porous, translucent, fine, resonant, that even steel cannot scratch. Until the end of the 17th century the properties of Kaolin remained a secret of the Chinese. Not until 1709 was it discovered by European ceramists.

Production did not begin in France until a stratum had been identified in 1768 at Saint Yrieix near Limoges.

The discovery of Kaolin in Lower Normandy in a town called Pieux (in the Cotentin) saw the start of manufacture at Valognes (Manche). The latter had financial problems and closed down in July 1812. Its manager Joachim Langlois decided to transfer the business to Bayeux where he set up in the old Benedictine convent, unused since the Revolution. He brought in some of his old work-force.

The proximity of Kaolin at Pieux, the presence of a good industrial and commercial tradition and the know-how of the local potters regarding ceramics allowed the firm to continue for almost a century and a half. After that, profound difficulties concerning the re-organisation after the last War led to the defnitive closure of the entreprise in 1951.

The story of porcelain in Bayeux can be told in three stages, associated with the names of families that headed its manufacture : the Langlois period (1812-1849), the Gosse period (1849-1878) and finally the Morlent period (1878-1951).

Each of them can be identified by their own style of decoration but the china produced was not all luxury porcelain, richly enhanced with coloured motifs but the importance, in the first place, was given by

Decorated plate in blue, red and gold by Louis Duval

Langlois and Gosse to white china, used in households daily, then, under Gosse and above all under Morlent, came the specialisation and the use of chemicals in their workshops.

One of the peculiarities of Bayeux porcelain lies in the composition of the Kaolin from Pieux. Its qualities were discovered early on, namely that from it a porcelain could be made that was durable and which could stand up to high temperature and sudden heat.

The mixture of Kaolin and chalk could be turned on the potters wheel or stamped out to size; it could also be diluted with water, poured into a mould to make pieces of different shapes. After drying when the pieces were heated at 800° (the warm-up) by which it was no.longer pliant. A piece not yet enamelled, could be decorated in a range of colours by using cobalt oxide for blue or chrome for green in a process known as reduced chromatic. It was then plunged into a bath of enamel consisting mainly of feldspath, or pegmatite (a form of crystalised granite), silica and chalk in suspension in water. It then went into the kiln again, heated at 1 410° (the firing). The heat and enclosed kiln cause the clay and the enamel to vitrify, the metalic oxide takes on the required colour tone (for example, black cobalt oxide, turns blue). Finally a further decoration in rich and varying colours can be put on the enamel and the piece is given a third firing at about 700°.

The makers of porcelain in Bayeux explored every possibility offered by these tehniques in an effort to develop a range of china that was both competitive and work of quality.

The porcelain pieces of Langlois stand out in the constant efforts for something new. The founder of the firm tried castors for beds, marine pulleys, capsules and crucibles for laboratories and placques for street

RUE DU GOULET

names. He also designed a form of artistic printing which he hoped would compete with the lithograph ; it was called, «caustographie». In his time as director, pieces of luxury china were quite numerous. At first the designs were mostly «Louis XVI» and «Directoire»; decoration was produced by «moufle» firing (where the pieces in the kiln had no contact with the flames). The motifs were in gold with fleurettes in polychrome. From 1820 onwards he used decorations in cobalt blue put in place before enamelling, alternatively with motifs in red and gold, the final firing being in «feu moufle». The decor in this period was largely influenced by china from the Far East. On the death of Joachim in 1830 the range of richly decorated porcelain gave way to greater production of white china destined for household use. Nevertheless some very fine pieces were produced in oriental style and in blue, red and gold, or in plain monochrome of cobalt blue, among which were some real chefs-oeuvre signed by the painter Louis Duval.

From the mid-nineteenth century, François Gosse underlined the commercial character of the firm from both a technical and economic stand-point. Production was then directed at supplying laboratories and from then on, as important as the output of household china. Decorated pieces were aimed at the household china market, the artists from then on, set to diversifying the variety of motifs in a very standardised range. The Far-Eastern decors were rapidly replaced. Red and gold disappeared to make way for a range, produced entire-

A jug for hot-chocolate from the François Gosse period

ly in «feu de moufle» with designs inspired not only by the Chinese but equally by Egypt and Ancient Greece.

At the same time, the firm produced a range of porcelain, an elaboration of their range in blue, not «moufle» but «grand feu». This was the final firing in the kiln, of a series called either : «à la pomme» or «fleur de pommier».

A set of china during Morlent's time known as : «à la Marguerite»

Under the Morlent family, the firm saw a considerable increase in indutrial china. Chemistry became their main target and finally amounted to 80% of the production. The decor «au feu de moufle» disappeared completely whilst household china had pride of place with typical elegant motifs. At first these were «à la fleur de pommier» (apple blossom) and «Saxe», turned out in the last third of the 19th century by Jules Morlent, followed by «à la Marguerite», very typical of the output in the first half of the 20th century. At the same period the firm began to produce china with their classic decor of «au barbeau» in blue and green. This also had the firing known as «grand feu». When the factory closed its gates in 1951, after a century and a half of activity, Bayeux was known throughout the world from Buenos Aires to Helsinki and from Sydney to Philadelphia ■

Porcelain produced for chemistry laboratories, in Morlent's time

Bayeux Lace

their benevolent establishments that would give employment to their pensioners and at the same time contribute to their own financial resources.

At the outset, lace-making began in a small way before really taking off during the 18th century. if only twenty-two girls were lace-makers in 1698, half a century later there were over two hundred. At the same time the craft spread across the City ; other workshops were started in the parishes of Saint-Malo, Saint-Loup, Saint-Patrice and de la Poterie. On the eve of the Revolution, lace-making had left behind it, the limits of charity institutions to rise to the level of real industry.

Traditionally, crafts taught by the nuns were in the nature of apprenticeship. The apprenticeship ended, the girls were given a «trousseau» and departed with a craft in their fingers to work at home, making contact with firms that would buy their handiwork. By 1874 therefore, bobbin-lace making was considered as the main industry of the City. It occupied over a thousand

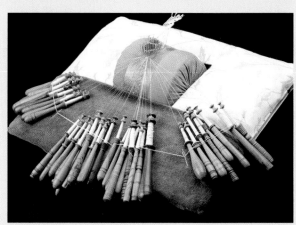

The craft of a lace-maker

lace-makers in the City and suburbs.

To make Bobbin-lace, the lace-maker uses what is known as a «carreau». In Bayeux this consisted of a revolving cylindrical cushion (drum), set in a square of wood that was cloth-covered. Attached to the cylinder are «fuseaux» : bobbins. These are thin with a haft attached, sometimes with a cover of horn (noquette) to protects the thread.

«Bourgeoise de Bayeux» (1848)
A middle-class lady painted by Hallot

Bobin Lace-making is a craft practised in Bayeux for three centuries. Monsignor Francis de Nesmond was hardly unaware of this when in 1676 he put the office of Assisted Children from the General Hospital, in the hands of two Sisters of Providence, an Order founded in Rouen about ten years earlier, that was keen to develop a craft that was to make Bayeux Lace-making world famous.

The Hospital administrators benefitted by a concession from Louis XIV in 1662 to open workshops in

A card attached to the drum showed the pattern the lace-maker was to follow. It was pierced with a multitude of holes in which to stick pins to hold the threads as they intercrossed. If the lace formed a continuous band, the drum continued to turn. The number of bobbins equalled the number of threads used in the pattern. This varied according to the size and complexity of the pattern. Large pieces of lace called for a number of bands, joined together later by lace-makers who specialised in that type of needlework.

During the period od the Revolution, the production of Bayeux lace underwent a radical change, notably after the dissolution of the Religious Communities in 1792. The industry developed independently of the Religious Orders, (in 1824 the number of firms involved amounted to over twenty-five ; Tardif and Carpentier-Delamare being the most prominent). Bayeux reached its zenith

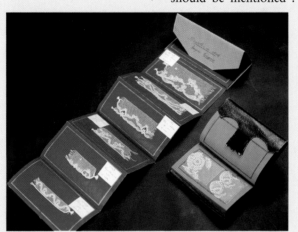

Books of samples from the firm Maison Lefébure c. 1880

economically in mid 19th century (accounting for 15 000 lace-makers in the City and its surroundings). Lace-making involved a great many different types of work : designers and the creation of motifs, those who prepared the card with holes corresponding to the pattern, agents who collected the lace. Needle-women who joined the bands of lace to make the finished product, commercial travellers for the lace firms and finally the lace-makers themselves, working mainly at home in a very precarious existence. Now no trace of the industry remains architecturally. The firms were generally in ordinary houses and therefore left no trace (see no. 14 Rue Saint-Jean, no. 35 Rue Général-de-Dais, no. 9 and 13 Impasse Prud'homme all of which housed successively the firm Maison Lefébure.

Confronted with inceased mechanisation that spelt the inexorable decline of Bayeux bobbin-lace making, the accent was more and more in the second half of the 19th century, on the ultra artistic, notably by work ordered for the «Compagnie des Indes» and the houses of Pagny and Lefébure, destined for the upper middle class.

Bayeux had certainly made a reputation for a type of bobbin-lace in white silk : a tradition that dated from the end of the 17th century, but the lace had greater fame for the diversity and quality of output. Among the finest pieces that came from Bayeux workshops, should be mentioned : black «Chantilly» lace for a finesse that went unequalled and the «blondes» of unbleached silk known as «blondes de Caen». Although bobbin-lace in its raw state, consisted of bands often as edging for frills or trimmings for ladies' clothing, it was also assembled as a whole garment : shawls, lace-caps and head-dresses, as well as forming part of other finery and used in umbrellas, sunshades and fans.

In the same way, in high quality lace, the Bayeux firm, Maison Lefébure continued until 1973, until there was no one left to succeed. The «Conservatoire de la Dentelle» (the Bayeux Lace Conservatory) at no. 6 Rue du Bienvenu, continues, not only the prodution by professional lace-makers among whom is Maître d'Art Mylène Salvador, but also with designs that latterly have been produced in collaboration with the Paris houses of «Haute couture française» (Balmain, Dior, Lapidus, Hermès and Christian Lacroix) or with contemporary artists such as Joan Creten, Maria Hahnenkamp, Ghada Hamer, Anette Messager or Christian Zimermmann ■

Air-raid shelter, Rue Saint-Quentin

On 3rd September 1939, France and the United Kingdom began the war against Germany. After nine months of «phoney war», on 18th June 1940, the same day as the historic Call-to-Arms by General de Gaulle over tha air-waves of the BBC, troops of the Third Reich entered Bayeux. So began a period of four years of occupation, restriction and distress.

The proximity of the coast made the Bessin a particularly sensitive military zone. Coastal defence was one of the priorities as far as the German Authorities were concerned who, denying access to the population, undertook from 1942 extensive works of fortification. In contrast to the «Pas de Calais», the work was confined to beach defences along which heavily fortified bunkers were erected, augmented by thousands of obstacles (mines, barbed wire and iron spikes...) embedded along the shore.

About ten kilometres north of Bayeux, the defences were re-inforced by the Battery at Longues-sur-Mer with its firing control post and four casemates with 150 mm guns having a range of 19 kms ; these are still in place today. In Bayeux itself, near the Red Cross Clinic, built in 1943, stands an air-raid shelter in re-inforced concrete, with about ten rooms for some twenty beds ; is was staffed by two medical officers and four medical orderlies. It is the last vestige that remains of the German occupation. The German Authorities requisitioned buildings for their administrative network such as the Kommandantur (the seat of local military administration), situated at no. 31 Rue aux Coqs and the Feldgendarmerie (German Military Police) installed in a hotel at the corner of Rue de la Juridiction and Rue des Cuisiniers.

It can be well understood the extent to which the gathering of intelligence on military coastal defence played in action undertaken by the local resistence network. Repression was pitiless and the toll was heavy since at least five people were shot and twenty-one resistants from the Bessin were deported. From further afield, of seventy deportees, almost half ended their days in the camps of Auschwitz, Bad-Oeynhaussen, Bergen-Belsen, Buchenwald, Dachau, Dora, Gros-Rosen, Hinzert, Natzwiller-Struthof, Neuengamme, Mathausen and Oranienburg-Schachsenhausen. It is in their memory that after the War, in Rue Larcher the monument by the sculptor Ulysse Genignani (1906-1973) was erected ; on which are inscribed some verses of Louis Aragon (1897-1982) taken from the «Rose et le Réséda».

Building in Rue des Cuisiniers taken over by the Feldgendarmerie

A detail from the Monument to the deportees Rue Larcher

General D.D. Eisenhower

In 1943 the Allies agreed on mounting an offensive on a broad front in France during the following summer. In the spring of 1944 the beaches of the Bessin were specifically marked out for military action on the most gigantesque scale history had ever known.

The heart of the operation began at dawn on 6th June 1944. Bayeux, the first sous-prefecture of Metropolitan France liberated, became the seat of provisional government in the French Republic, set up by General de Gaulle in person, as from 14th June. Bayeux has therefore a double claim to the title of the places symbolising Europe's regained freedom, which each museum in its own way recalls : The Battle of Normandy Museum (Bd Fabian Ware) and The General de Gaulle Museum (8 Rue Bourbesneur).

The combined GHQ (Anglo-American) was placed under the supreme command in 1943 of General Dwight D. Eisenhower to whom the City of Bayeux chose to render homage in 1994 by the erection of a monument at the eastern entrance to the City (work of the American sculptor Robert Dean) for his careful preparation of the Landings. This took in the Orne estuary to the outlet of the Vire, zones defended by the 716th and the 352nd German infantry divisions, in all about 15 000 men. The Allied ground troops were commanded by General Bernard Law Montgomery, consisting mainly of British and American soldiers with contingents of Canadians, Australians, South-Africans, New-Zealanders, Northern-Irish, as well as Free-French, Belgians, Poles, Czechs, Dutch and Norwegians. The objective was to establish a bridge-head and put in place an infra-structure (artificial ports, air-fields, road-works) allowing a sound logistic back-up (movement of vehicles, petrol, armaments and food...) vital to the success of the operation.

During the night of 5th to 6th June nearly 7 000 ships under the command of Admiral Bertram H. Ramsay crossed the Channel with 133 000 men on board ready to disembark. The first assault waves landed on the beaches beween 06.30 and 07.25 at five points : to west, in the American sector (UTAH and OMAHA) under the orders of General Omar Bradley and to the east (GOLD JUNO and SWORD) under the orders of General Miles Dempsey. These were preceded by raids inland by units of Airborne troops, notably at Sainte-Mère-Eglise and at Ranville (23 000 paratroops dropped in Normandy on 6th June). The Allied Air Force commanded by Air-Marshall Trafford Leign-Malory, played a vital role throughout D-Day, dropping 10 000 tons of bombs on German defences and on the main axes of communications in the region. In an extraordinary fashion at less than 10 kms from Gold Beach (beaches of Asnelles and Ver-sur-Mer) under attack by 38 000 men of 50th Northumbrian British Division, Bayeux came out unscathed, a miracle. Thought to be due, by some in Bayeux, to Our Lady to whom a monument was dedicated in 1947, the work of Fr. M. Bernard (Rue Maurice-Schumann).

Commemorative Plaque in honour of 56th British Independent Infantry Brigade
(The lower north side of the Cathedral)

Monument dedicated to Our Lady, Rue Maurice-Schumann

The City, in the hands of British troops of 56th Independent Brigade from 8 p.m. hours on the 6th June was liberated the following morning. In Rue Lambert-Leforestier near the gateway of the Deanery and also on the lower north-side of the Cathedral entrance, two plaques commemorate respectively the men of the 50th Division and the 56th Brigade to whom Bayeux owed its liberation.

Battle of Normandy Museum Bd Fabian Ware

The Mission of 50th Division was, notably to take the Battery at Longues-sur-Mer, invest the City of Bayeux and control Route Nationale 13 to the east of the City, and finally to join up with the Americans at Port-en-Bessin. The latter was not accomplished by the evening of 6th June. The Germans at Port-en-Bessin held out and the difficulties encountered by 1st American Division, «The Big Red One» were huge ; to hold the shore and establish a bridge-head a kilometre and a half deep inland. Losses were considerable : 3 000 dead and 3 000 wounded or missing.

As the Battle of Normandy Museum shows, action on 6th June was far from the final victory. The Museum has on display a collection of quite exceptional exhibits, arranged both chronologically and by theme (uniforms, equipment, arms and vehicles in use at the time, as well as photographs, notices and newpapers...) together with numerous personal belongings and souvenirs from men who spent 77 days on the ground in Lower Normandy. Fierce fighting continued until the end of August when Field-Marshal Erwin Rommel's troops were encircled in the Falaise Pocket.

In this context, the artificial port of Arromanches, to the north of Bayeux constructed between the 9th ahd 18th June, played an important role until the port of Cherbourg was put into service, two months after liberation of the town on 27th June. From June to August 1944, 20% of the traffic and cargo discharged between the two strands of the Manche, came from the quays of Cherbourg, that is : over 200 000 men, 500 000 tons of war material and 40 000 vehicles of which almost 3 000 were tanks. At the same, the little fishing port of Port-en-Bessin was rapidly transformed into a real oil terminal.

To facilitate transport, the British Royal Engineers built during enemy action, the Bayeux ring-road (the By-pass) making possible from 24th June onwards the passage of army convoys and avoiding the passage by army vehicles through the tortuous streets of the old city. Thanks to this infra-structure, still in place, the City became a refuge for the civil population, fleeing the fighting ; it also became an army-hospital base with three centres of tri for the wounded and five large army-hospitals. Army-quarters multiplied, a POW camp was opened in Saint-Vigor-le-Grand and Bayeux became a tourist centre where men could relax for a few hours away from the Front. There was no chance of seeing the Bayeux Tapestry which had left the City in 1941 for safe-keeping at a depot for exhibits from National Museums at Château de Sourches (Sarthe). At the end of June 1944 it was taken to the Musée du Louvre in Paris, from where the Nazis attempted to take it, on 21st August but were impeded by the street fighting.

Invited by Winston Chuchill to visit the Bridge-head, General de Gaulle with a dozen companions disembarked from the MTP «Combattante» on 14th June 1944 on the beach at Graye-sur-Mer. He was greeted by Maurice Schumann who had on 6th June to arrange a liaison with the «Résistance» in the Bessin and prepare for the General's arrival. The monument erected at the western gates of the City, work of the sculptor Raoul Lamouredieu, commemorates both the

Allied Landings and the welcome given to General de Gaulle by the people of Bayeux on the afternoon of 14th June.
The enthusiastic fervour by the people who surrounded him at four o'clock that

General de Gaulle in Bayeux
14th June 1944

afternoon was proof of his popularity and of the legitimacy of his position as head of Free France.

He went up, hemmed in by the crowd, Rue Saint-Martin and Rue Saint-Malo to Rue Général-de-Dais to enter the Sous-Prefecture. On the square were several

thousand people, come to listen to a short address, a speech to affirm the presence of France among her Allies.

He was greeted equally warmly at Isigny then Grandcamp before going back on board the «Combattante» that night to return to England.

De Gaulle's objective was essantially political. It was to make evident as quickly as possible on liberated territory the legitimacy of the Republic. To achieve this he chose the Sous-Préfecture of Bayeux to set up the headquarters of provisional government for the liberated territories. François Coulet his former head of Cabinet 1941 to 1942 appointed as from 12th June Regional Commissioner of the Republic for Normandy, assisted him in carrying this out. A monument in bronze in the coutyard of the Sous-Préfecture and an inscription engraved in the wall of the courtyard both record the event.

The powers of the Commissioner of the Republic were wide, they allowed François Coulet to govern the liberated territories under his authority. With the support of his two «Chargés de Mission», Geoffroy de Courcel and Pierre Laroque, the new Sous-Préfet whom he had just appointed, Raymond Triboulet and members of the Liberation Comitee ; he soon made clear his capacities as an administrator and brought pressure to bear on Allied Services in charge of civil matters. The task of François Coulet, in charge at Bayeux until 1st September 1944, was difficult and wide in its scope : the removal and dismissal of civil or elected officials, the appointment of new ones, organising the reception of refugees, food supplies... Press publications, suspended from early June were re-established in Bayeux when the first issue appeared of «Renaissance du Bessin» dated 23rd June 1944, a twice-weekly that became the organ of official publications of decrees or decisions taken by the Authorities (suspension of certain laws promulgated by the Vichy government and the dissolution of groups of collaborationists...).

For several weeks, until the liberation of Caen on 18th July, then Paris on 24th August, Bayeux was the administrative and political centre of Liberated France.

The 16th June 1946 was the date of the erection of a monument commemorating the speech given two years earlier (erected under the leafy foliage on Place Charles de Gaulle). The General in his historic discourse, in the course of which he made clear his thoughts on the institutions he considered necessary in France and which were those of the 1958 Constitution, mentions this period in the summer of 1944 in these terms : «*(...) It is here on the soil of our ancestors that our Sovereinty has come back to us ; (...) a sovereignty capable of re-establishing around it, National Unity and Imperial Unity, to gather all the forces of our Native Land and the Union Française, to carry on to final victory in common with the Allies, to deal as equals with other great nations, to maintain public order, to administer Justice and begin the work of reconstruction.*» Until 25th August 1944, Lower Normandy was a theatre of war and bloody battles, on the sequel of which rested the destiny of Europe. Unlike Bayeux, the only place in Normandy having offered no resistance and suffered no damage, the liberation unfolded throughout the region in blood and ruins. By the end of the month of August, of the two million troops that crossed the Channel, of which 1 200 000 were Americans, more than 200 000 were killed, wounded or missing. German losses were estimated at 240 000 and over 200 000 prisoners. Amongst the population of Lower Normandy over 12 000 civilians were killed. Bayeux was, of course greatly concerned and involved in the memory of the sacrifices of the men and women who died on the soil of Normandy. On one side of the By-pass, opposite The Battle of Normandy Museum is the largest Commonwealth military cemetery of the last War. There are, in all, the graves of 4 648 soldiers who fell in battle, of which are : 3 953 British, 181 Canadians, 17 Australians, 8 New-Zealanders, 1 South African but also 25 Poles, 3 French, 2 Italians, 7 Russians and 446 Germans. Opposite is a memorial erected to the memory of : 1 8070 British, 270 Canadians and 15 South Africans killed during the Battle of Normandy who have no known grave. Saved from the destruction of war, the City has underdone a rapid expansion in the last fifty years largely due to the By-pass. The By-pass today is a boulevard skirting the City. It has preserved its historic heart, that has a surface of 80 hectares, green belt safe-garded in 1971 by Ministerial Decree. So that, the value added to the heritage of this old Norman City is without doubt, the finest homage the people of Bayeux can offer to those who gave their lives ; a sacrifice that Justice and Freedom might triumph ■

E ven in the heart of the City when the coach-gates are ajar one notices that many homes have gardens, carefully tended. This dimension is noticeable too in the numerous spaces of lawn and flower-beds that predominate.

Former workshop on «Square de l'Ilet»

The banks of the Aure

For the visitor, the banks of the Aure that meander across Bayeux from south to north, provide the chance of a stroll to discover one of the most intimate parts of the City. The path of the river arranged in the course of the centuries for work or pleasure is in fact, dotted with countless elements that illustrate the daily life that occupied the people of Bayeux in times past.

At the southern entrance of the City, the river with its banks high and dry, green and bordered with poplars maintains the bucolic character of the trail it traces through the Bessin countryside. Further, alongside the Parc Michel d'Ornano, one can see on the bank opposite, through the foliage of Weeping Willows, the first signs of the work-a-day,

The Aure seen from Pont Saint-Jean

(world of other days) such as a wash-house for laundresses or the paved descent gently sloping to the waters edge, where the horses quenched their thirst, at a time when equestrian transport reigned supreme in the City. A little further on, the first barrage; here the flow of water was canalised to turn the mill-wheel at Croquevieille, one of Bayeux's many water-mills.

The river then passes under the old Hôtel-Dieu, it then dividees ; its two paths mark out the end of the Convent garden of the Augustine nuns charged with the running of the hospice until the Revolution.

A bridge, lately built, permits access to the bushy islet thus formed. One becomes aware that buildings form the bank of a narrow canal ending in a sluice. Beyond is the mill-race diverting the river towards a mill. Several houses bear the trace of a former workshop : wash-house or drying-house for dyers or tanners.

Other signs of former crafts typical of Bayeux in bygone days can be senn beyond the pont Saint-Jean where the old fish-market stood. One can follow the river after the mill at the «Place aux Pommes», all along the Pierre Villion promenade. On the opposite bank is the Rue des Teinturiers called also in Medieval times, Rue de la Tannerie. Beyond this the river crosses the old market-gardens and after the mill, «Moulin Renard» flows on through the Bessin countryside.

The attractive «Place de Gaulle»

The «Place de Gaulle» is now one of the loveliest squares in the heart of the City. It is an extremely attractive urban open space. A vast quadrangle of undeniable beauty, set in a framework of paved streets, it is bordered by elegant houses built in the 18th and 19th centuries. In the south-west corner stands the former convent of the Benedictine nuns, founded in the middle of the 17th century and which, from 1812 to 1951 was used for the making of porcelain. In front of it is a monument dedicated in 1908 to the soldiers in the War of 1870, the work of the sculptor A. Le Duc (1848-1918). In the opposite corner at the entrance to the prestigious Rue Général-de-Dais stands the statue of the Bayeux poet Alain Chartier (1358-1433) the work of a Morlaix sculptor, dated 1947.

A lavoir (wash-house) on the banks of the Aure Parc Michel d'Ornano

At the end of the 19th century and beginning of the 20th the Square was the site of the main public festivals organised by the Municipality with gun salutes, fireworks and ascents for the public in a captive air-balloon, notably in the festivities of the 14th July. At the beginning of the 20th century it was also the place of the «Hiring-day» for farm-servants on the first Sunday after the 4th July. Once hired the agricultural workers were engaged for a year, by local farmers.

Before the War, the Square was called «Place du Château» : an allusion to the medieval castle that once stood on the site. The fort : a square tower with eight turrets was taken down from 1773 onwards by order of Louis XVI.

Place Charles de Gaulle

Not until 1840 was there a real attempt to lay out the Square. In that year the area was levelled and became a vast carpet of green within a framework of Lime-trees, that gave the Square such charm. In 1888 a fountain was erected in the centre of it. Tradition has it, that the statue on the fountain allegorically representing the City (the work of the sculptor E. Décorchemont), but resembling Melle Niobey (daughter of the donor of the fountain) was meant to be Popée, the young girl whom Rollo took for his wife.

The Sous-Préfecture adds an official and historical dimension to the Square. The building, built in 1863, is in fact the place where the sovereignty of Republican France was re-established in 1994. Under the leafy foliage on the eastern side of the Square, a simple monument has been erected recalling that, on this spot, Général de Gaulle spoke for the first time on the soil of Liberated France, on 14th June 1944.

The Botannical Garden

The Botannical garden

Among the places preferred for a walk or stroll by the people of Bayeux the «Jardin Botanique» holds a privileged place. The creation of this landscape park of 2.6 hectares on the northern outskirts of the City on Route no.. 55 to Port-en-Bessin, was due to the initiative of Charlemagne Jean-Delamare (1772-1858) who contributed financially but never lived to see it. It was Eugène Bühler (1822-1907) and his brother Denis who designed the «Parc de la tête d'or» in Lyon in 1856 who were given the task of planning a «public garden» for Bayeux, in 1859. Since that date very few changes had been made. The park is surrounded by a screen of trees and bushes. There are two entrances that give on to alleya with gentle and elegant curves from which are numerous views. Skirting the three central lawns they lead on through elaborate landscaping on which the architect has created screens of greenery with wooded rises and rockery, with lone trees that high-light the panorama. The main species of trees and bushes planted between 1859 and 1864 (chestnut, pines, plane-trees, holly, maple, limes, sophoras, yews, beech, catalpa, Norwegian pines, acacias, cedars or nut trees) are there still and in the proportions equivalent to the scheme of Eugène Bühler. Among the 400 trees still in the park the most spectacular is witout doubt the Weeping Beech (Fagus sylvatica «Pendula»), classed as a natural monument since 1932, the top of which is as much as 40 metres in diameter ■

Markets, Good food and th

Bayeux's identity has, progressively been formed, in its long history of two thousand years and has amounted to richesse and renown. We have here, step by step throughout its long and diverse heritage, tried to assess its qualities ; there is however another way to mark out the most striking factors. All through the year, a series of events demonstrate the extent to which the Bajocasses are attached to them, celebrate them and enlarge on , the most typical aspects. The identity of Bayeux is first of all bound up with the rich earth of agricultural renown. Capital of the Bessin, it has long been reputed for first quality dairy products in France. It can equally pride itself, along with the Basque country, Corsica, Gascony or Limousin as well known for one of the six local breeds of pigs of national repute. With farm products menaced with extinction not long ago, the Bayeux breed of pigs has escaped industrial methods of production.

The arrival of little white piglets with black patches, so plentiful at one time on the Tuesday market is today a great event. So that every year in October their presence on the occasion of the «Fête du goût» «food of taste» festival, attracts a large number of professionals, amateurs and the simply curious.

It can be claimed that the «Fête du goût» continues throughout the year on the Bayeux Saturday market ; a market listed among the hundred exceptionally good markets in France for the high quality of the products on sale.

On Saturday, Place Saint-Patrice presents a virtual invitation to the pleasures of the table. In the Bessin, shell-fish, crabs and lobsters are of first quality. All the diversity of «fruits de la mer» is here, being so close to the coast. (oysters from Isigny or from Courseulles, coquilles Saint-Jacques, lobsters, crabs of all kinds, shrimps, bass, conger-eels and sole from Port-en-Bessin or Grandcamp).

There are live fowls destined for farmyards and poultry-keepers (cockerels, pullets, young chicks, guinea-fowl, geese, ducklings and young rabbits) that attract young children.

There is farm produce from local producers (grain-fed fowls, fresh eggs, cream, butter and cheese from non-pasteurised full-cream milk) all of which make traditional Norman cuisine famous.

The taste of unctuous fresh cream leads on to the

perfume of the apple. Cider (the juice of fermented fresh apples), Calvados (apple-jack or the eau-de-vie of cider), pommeau (a blending of Calvados and apple-juice) are retailed on the market.

On green-grocers stalls are fresh vegetables grown locally, butchers and pork-butchers sell black-puddings and also white-puddings, tripe and a speciality from Vire : andouilles, with also a variety of cooked-meats and patés. Competitions are held, notably for the finest tripe but also for other specialities, for which there is keen competition not only between market stall-holders and butchers in shops but by roundsmen who make these delicaties too.

In the sphere of bread and pastry, «brié» falls somewhere between the two ; it is dense and rich in taste. The «brioche» obtained from the baker, must for people of the Bessin be a «fallue», made with butter. A favourite dish, much beloved by visitors to the region who like rice-pudding is «teurgoule» : rice-pudding flavoured with cinnamon and well cooked, very familiar to the tables of the Bessin since the 18th century when it was permitted in the King's name when the grain harvest failed ■

Bayeux in festive mood

It is clear, merely from the presence of its famous Tapestry, the attachment Bayeux has to its medieval past. It is easy to imagine therefore the enthusiasm in 1924 for the millenary celebrations of the founding of the Duchy of Normandy and more recently in July 1977 the ninth centenary, heralded by sumptuous celebrations.

In 1987, on the occasion of the ninth centenary of the death of William the Conqueror, a medieval market was held, which, in view of its popularity has become an annual event and takes place on the first week-end in July. From then on these medieval festivities have become vertual pageants, taking up all the streets around the Cathedral, using the combined efforts of several hundreds of Bayeux people in costume for the day, with some professional actors.

Jugglers, musicians, actors, horsemen, gentle ladies and knights, pour into the streets, a tumultuous throng, craftsmen trying to draw customers to their stalls, those making roasts trying to draw people to their taverns. All the while the master stone-masons, glaziers, wrought-iron smiths and carpenters, busy themselves with their work on the Cathedral, whilst the exhibition of medieval books holds sway as the great and small, crowd in. As night falls there rises a fairy-like spectacle of light and sound.

Medieval festivities

Medieval Bayeux, at the very heart of the 1944 Landings, from then on became one of the symbols of Europe set free.

The City is, in the nature of events, entrusted with a mission to keep alive the memory and pass on to the future generation the sacrifice of those men and women to whom is owed its liberation on the morning of the 7th June. To this end, take place the many commemorations held each year at the beginning of June, throughout the region of which Bayeux is capital.

Over the past decades, Bayeux has had the honour of welcoming very many people of note, from the world over, from heads of State or Government, veterans of the last War, and ordinary citizens. Holding dear, those moments lived through, in June 1944, some tragic, though others of intense joy, there have been moments of merriment too, when our people in a festive mood have welcomed their distinguised visitors.

In the desire to continue in the role that history has handed down, the City wishes to cotinue in the service of freedom and democracy, in rendering homage annually to journalists the world over, who expose themselves to danger, whether civil or military in the exercise of their profession, often at the peril of their lives. «The Bayeux Prize for War Correspondants» consists of seven trophies, presented every October since 1994. It is an international event in which the public take a large part, particularly in the exhibitions mounted for the occasion, debates and film shows.

These major events in the Bayeux Calendar of celebrations is of course just one part of vast programme of activities and peak occasions for public pleasure and in which to join, whether it be culturally or in the domain of sport. Each, in its own way, demonstrates that Bayeux, a City rich in tradition is a generous City, with its gates wide open to the world and to the future ■

Medieval festivities

Concert in the gardens of the Deanery

67

Bibliography

Bayeux. Art de Basse-Normandie, numéro spécial, n°54, 1969.

VERNEY Antoine – Les Collections préhistoriques du Musée de Bayeux. Bayeux,
Musée Baron Gérard ed., collection Notes et documents du Musée,1994.

BERTRAND Simone, LEMAGNEN Sylvette – La Tapisserie de Bayeux, Rennes,
Editions Ouest-France, 1996.

IXe centenaire de la cathédrale de Bayeux. Art de Basse-Normandie n°76, hiver 1978-1979.

BERTRAND Simone, LE CARPENTIER Marc – Bayeux Médiéval. Bayeux, Editions Heimdal, 1976.

NEVEUX François – Bayeux et Lisieux villes épiscopales de Normandie à la fin du Moyen Age. Caen,
Editions du Lys, 1996.

MARIE Abbé Jean – Bayeux ville d'art. 2 volumes, Bayeux 1969.

EL KORDI Mohamed – Bayeux aux XVIIe-XVIIIe siècles, contribution à l'histoire urbaine de la France,
La Haye - Paris, Mouton & co. – Ecole pratique des hautes études eds., 1970.

HUET Christiane – Bayeux au siècle des Lumières. Embellissements, urbanisme et architecture
au XVIIIe siècle. Paris, Editions la Mandragore, 2001.

HUFTON Olwen H. – Bayeux in the late eighteen century, a social study. Oxford,
The Clarendon Press ed. 1967.

MICHEL Edmond – Monographie d'un canton type (Bayeux). Paris-Nancy,
Berger-Levrault Editeurs, 1911.

Bayeux et le Bessin 1940-1944. Vie quotidienne. Résistance. Déportation. Libération. Evrecy-Bayeux, 1996.

LEGOUT Gérard – Le Jour J et la bataille de Normandie. Cully, Editions Orep, 1998.

DECAUMONT, Françoise (dir.) - Le discours de Bayeux, hier et aujourd'hui. Colloque de Bayeux,
15 juin 1990, Paris, Economica Ed., 1991.

VERNEY Antoine, HEROUARD Dominique, MATOÏAN Valérie, Le Musée Baron Gérard de Bayeux ou
l'histoire d'une collection. Art de Basse-Normandie n°123, 2000.

LEJEUNE Jean – Les anciennes manufactures de porcelaine de Basse-Normandie. Valognes, Bayeux, Isigny,
Caen, 2ème édition, Cherbourg, La Dépêche, 1985.

BIANQUIS Laurent – Cuisine normande. Paris, Hachette, Petits pratiques hachette, 1998.

The reader desirous of deepening his knowledge of the history and heritage of Bayeux may usefully consult the
«Mémoires and Bulletins» published regularly since 1841 by the «Société de Sciences», «Arts et Belles-Lettres
de Bayeux». If he so wishes he may contact the Association at the following address : S.A.B.L., B.P. 46408 14404
Bayeux.

Bayeux Cathedral, seen from Rue Nesmond circa 1850 by A. Le Coulteux de Vertron (Baron Gérard Museum) ▶

INDEX OF THE STREETS, SITES AND PRINCIPAL MONUMENTS MENTIONED IN THE TEXT

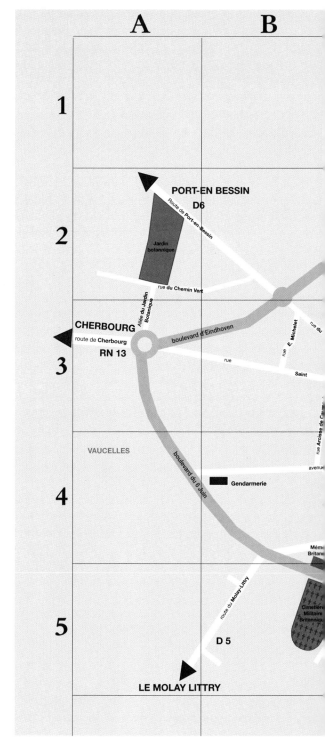

Our grateful thanks for the photographs appearing in this work, go to the following :
Antoine Verney - David Lemaresquier - Eric Marie - L'Image de Marc' Bayeux
The City of Bayeux© - (photo library of the Baron Gérard Museum).
Extracts from the 11th century Bayeux Tapestry by special permission of the City of Bayeux

The Author and Publisher wish to thank :
The City of Bayeux - Catherine Duncombe - Dominique Hérouard - Jean-Marc Héroult
Valérie Matoïan - Sandrine Pierre

EDITIONS
OREP

15, rue de Largerie - 14480 Cully
Normandie - France
Tél. (33) 02 31 08 31 08
Fax (33) 02 31 08 31 09
info@orep-pub.com

Graphic Design : OREP
ISBN : 2-912925-31-2
Copyright OREP 2002
Filed officially by OREP Autumn 2002